Other Books by Reuben Fine

THE PERSONALITY OF THE ASTHMATIC CHILD
THE DEVELOPMENT OF FREUD'S THOUGHT
THE PSYCHOLOGY OF THE CHESS PLAYER
PSYCHOANALYTIC PSYCHOLOGY
THE DEVELOPMENT OF PSYCHOANALYTIC THOUGHT
THE INTIMATE HOUR
THE PSYCHOANALYTIC VISION
THE HEALING OF THE MIND
THE LOGIC OF PSYCHOLOGY
THE MEANING OF LOVE IN HUMAN EXPERIENCE
THE FORGOTTEN MAN
TROUBLED MEN
NARCISSISM, THE SELF, AND SOCIETY
THE HISTORY OF PSYCHOANALYSIS (new, expanded edition)
THE BORDERLINE PATIENT
LOVE AND WORK

TROUBLED WOMEN

Reuben Fine

TROUBLED WOMEN

Roles and
Realities in
Psychoanalytic
Perspective

 Jossey-Bass Publishers • San Francisco

Copyright © 1992 by Jossey-Bass Inc., Publishers, 350 Sansome Street, San Francisco, California 94104. Copyright under International, Pan American, and Universal Copyright Conventions. All rights reserved. No part of this book may be reproduced in any form—except for brief quotation (not to exceed 1,000 words) in a review or professional work—without permission in writing from the publishers.

For sales outside the United States contact Maxwell/Macmillan International Publishing Group, 866 Third Avenue, New York, New York 10022

Printed on acid-free paper and manufactured in the United States of America

 The paper used in this book meets the State of California requirements for recycled paper (50 percent recycled waste, including 10 percent postconsumer waste), which are the strictest guidelines for recycled paper currently in use in the United States.

Library of Congress Cataloging-in-Publication Data

Fine, Reuben, date.
    Troubled women : roles and realities in psychoanalytic perspective / Reuben Fine. — 1st ed.
      p.   cm.—(The Jossey-Bass social and behavioral science series)
    Includes bibliographical references (p.) and index.
    ISBN 1-55542-408-2 (acid-free paper)
    1. Women—Psychology. 2. Women—Socialization. 3. Femininity (Psychology) 4. Women and psychoanalysis. 5. Happiness.
I. Title.   II. Series.
HQ1206.F466   1992
155.6'33—dc 20   91-35629
                                                                     CIP

FIRST EDITION
HB Printing   10 9 8 7 6 5 4 3 2 1   *Code 9213*

The Jossey-Bass
Social and Behavioral Science Series

CONTENTS

	Preface	xi
	The Author	xv
1.	The Attack on the Traditional Role	1
2.	Psychoanalysis and Women's Liberation	13
3.	Love	24
4.	Sexuality	38
5.	Motherhood	56
6.	Separation from the Father	70
7.	The Entertainer	86
8.	Attachment and Loss	99
9.	The Single Woman	114
10.	The Divorced Woman	131
11.	Recapitulation	145
12.	The New Woman	153

References 157

Index 163

PREFACE

When I began thinking about a companion work to *Troubled Men,* the natural topic was women. Freud's famous question—What does a woman want?—has been echoed and reechoed throughout history. Many answers have been forthcoming, but all raise an even more fundamental question: What is inherent in being a woman? In this book, on the basis of numerous case histories as well as a study of the literature, I have offered an answer to this question.

In psychoanalysis I have formulated the problem in terms of the analytic ideal, which states that any woman or man attains the greatest degree of happiness if she or he is able to love, has a healthy sex life, has pleasure in general (rather than pain), has feelings yet is guided by reason, is part of a family, is part of the social order, enjoys work, can communicate, has creative outlets, and is free from psychiatric symptomatology.

Looked at in this way, psychoanalysis represents a theory of happiness that makes sense to a large number of human beings. It cuts through political systems and economic arrangements to get to the heart of what makes human beings happy. Many instances have been cited in the text where defiance of this fundamental order has led to much unhappiness, while obedience to this scheme leads to much happiness.

Women are made, not born, and how they are made depends most heavily on the circumstances of their parents' lives. I adhere strictly to Freudian theory, that the kind of woman a woman becomes can be gauged most directly from her sources, from the influences that helped to shape her in the early part of her life. I do not feel it necessary to hold on to some purely artificial theory of what women and men are, as many feminists seem to wish to do. That this is not the usual image of Freudian theory is a fact that I can deplore but cannot correct.

In its more scientific aspect, the women's liberation literature says essentially the same things (see Chodorow's *Feminism and Psychoanalysis*).

I present numerous clinical illustrations in this book to demonstrate how change can be effected in practice. The names of the individuals described in the cases have been changed to preserve anonymity. In addition, the details of the clinical material have been changed in nonessential ways to protect the identities of the individuals involved. No direct reference to any particular person is intended or implied.

Overview of the Contents

Chapter One provides a historical overview of men's attempts to define women's role in society—attempts that have been little more than methods of rationalizing the mistreatment of women. For the most part, men's views of women have been grossly distorted by the assumption that women are innately inferior to men. Since the eighteenth century, women's struggles for control of their lives have centered on the attack on this innatist view. As this chapter shows, the advent of psychoanalysis in the late nineteenth century gave women new ammunition in the fight for equality.

As the discussion in Chapter Two shows, the ends of women's liberation and psychoanalysis are essentially the same: liberation of the woman to achieve her own destiny. However, feminists have shortchanged many women by leaving marriage and motherhood out of the equation. The psychoanalytic ideal is to pursue the best solution for the individual woman, rather than for all women.

It is generally considered that love is more important to women than to men, especially romantic love. Chapter Three traces the problems women can have with love, including love for the mother, adolescent love, and romantic love. Contradictory aspects of love are examined as well.

Although love cannot truly be separated from sexuality, it

Preface xiii

can be useful to consider them in isolation from one another. Chapter Four begins with an overview of Western attitudes (mostly repressive) toward female sexuality and goes on to examine the range of sexual problems that are presented in analysis, including rejection of sex, the adjustment neurosis, promiscuity and sexual experimentation, and sex for the older woman.

The biological basis of womanhood is the capacity to bear children. If this capacity is thwarted, it can lead to serious consequences for the woman. Chapter Five examines a variety of the problems women can face in becoming mothers.

The woman's first attachment is to her mother; the second is to her father. Chapter Six explores the consequences for the girl of inability to detach herself from her early love for her father. Problems can arise if the father is too seductive toward his daughter, but they are equally possible if he is too distant or passive.

Chapter Seven examines the phenomenon of the entertainer as a consequence of inability to get over early attachment to the father. Many women performers (actresses, singers, and dancers) spend their whole lives trying to please their fathers by entertaining surrogate fathers (the audience). However, it is possible for entertainers to mature past this extreme attachment to the father.

Once a woman has separated herself from her mother and father, many other attachments (and losses) become possible. Desertion, death, sudden life shifts (such as marriage), and birth make up the bulk of such situations. Chapter Eight shows how inability to handle these attachments and losses can make it impossible for a woman to lead a healthy life.

Since societies are traditionally organized around marriage, single women commonly face social and psychological difficulties. Chapter Nine begins with an overview of the financial difficulties faced by the single woman today and proceeds to an examination of how the single woman can combine love and work in her life. Needless to say, the issue of when and if to have children is a major one for the single woman.

Similar problems are faced by the divorced woman, whose situation is the subject of Chapter Ten. Many divorced women feel very bitter toward men following their divorce, and this anger can cause all kinds of difficulties in their lives. This chapter also examines the issue of extramarital sex, which is often a major factor in a divorce.

Chapter Eleven is a recapitulation of the analytic ideal for women's lives and an examination of how this ideal helps them live in a healthy fashion. Three women's lives are probed in depth to illuminate the origins of their psychological problems and their resolution of those problems.

Chapter Twelve turns again to the basic questions posed by this book: What is inherent in being a woman? What does it take to be fulfilled as a woman? The failure of the women's movement to set up an ideal broad enough for all women is treated in more depth, and it becomes clear that it is through psychoanalysis rather than feminism that the individual woman can most effectively find her way to a healthy life.

I wish to express my thanks to my wife Marcia for her constant encouragement and persistence, as well as to my secretary for her expert typing of the manuscript.

New York, New York Reuben Fine
December 1991

THE AUTHOR

REUBEN FINE is a psychotherapist in private practice in New York City and director of the Consultation Center. Formerly, he was visiting professor at Adelphi University, director of the Center for Creative Living, and director of the New York Center for Psychoanalytic Training. He received his B.S. (1933) and M.S. (1939) degrees from the City University of New York, and his Ph.D. degree (1948) in clinical psychology from the University of Southern California.

Fine has long been active in the American Psychological Association (APA) and has been an APA fellow since 1955. He was president of the division of psychotherapy (1966-1967), a member of the council of representatives (1968-1970 and 1980-1983), and organizer and first president of the division of psychoanalysis (1979).

The author of numerous books, the latest of which is *Troubled Men* (1988), Fine also has served on a number of editorial boards and as consulting and honorary editor of such journals as *Psychotherapy, Book Forum, History of Childhood Quarterly, Journal of Psychoanalytic Psychology,* and *Current Issues in Psychoanalytic Practice.*

TROUBLED WOMEN

1 | The Attack on the Traditional Role

From time immemorial, women have been seen as inferior to men in most societies. Greek and Roman authorities took the male as the standard and saw the female as an inferior variation. In his treatise on reproduction, Aristotle wrote that the female is as it were a deformed male and stated that the menstrual discharge is semen, though in an impure condition. The second century Greek physician Galen even argued, if it can be called that, that women were men turned outside in. (The ovaries, in this view, were smaller, less perfect testes.)

The ancients further claimed that the womb wandered around the body. The womb, according to Plato, when remaining unfruitful long beyond its proper time, gets discontented and angry, and wandering in every direction through the body, closes up the passages of the breath, and by obstructing respiration, drives them to extremity causing all varieties of disease. The notion that the wandering uterus causes all manner of diseases in the woman's body lingered on until the twentieth century, when it was finally demolished by Freud and his contemporaries.

The image of the woman's body as inadequate has persisted right into modern times. In nineteenth century America, for example, woman was seen as inherently weak, with the major seat of her weakness being the sexual apparatus, particularly the vagina. Various devices were invented to cure the "sick" vagina, including such horrible methods as applying leeches to the woman's private parts.

How have these erroneous views about women and women's bodies gained ground and sustained themselves over the centuries?

In their book, *The Search for Woman*, which traces the evolution of ideas about the nature of women, H. C. Marlow and H. M. Davis argue that Christianity played a powerful role in this process.

First came the influence of the early Christian Fathers. In their view, women were intrinsically evil and men ought to avoid them; when men were unable to do so, the Fathers advised them to assert sufficient authority over women for self-protection. The Church Fathers frowned on marriage because during the act of sexual intercourse a man could not pray or receive the sacrament. Although Jerome did not actually condemn marriage, he subordinated it to virginity and widowhood. Tertullian, however, called women the devil's gateway through which death entered the world. Origen even had himself castrated to free himself from the temptations of the flesh.

Obviously these Church Fathers were seriously disturbed men, and their hatred of women had disastrous consequences for the world when the Church became a dominant power in the Middle Ages. Hildebrand, a monk who spent his life promoting chastity among men, especially the clergy, was known as a man filled with hatred and ambition.

The Dominance of Innatism

Olive Dunbar, a feminist and free-lance writer, believes that the various theories about women have left them without a well-defined role and mankind without general agreement on the nature of women. At various times and places—sometimes even simultaneously—women have been treated as a superhuman, an instrument for pleasure, a thing of evil, a household servant, or a superbly egocentric being. Greenson writes that the struggle for identification is more difficult for women than for men because of the hatred women have been subjected to in the past (Greenson, 1978).

In the seventeenth and eighteenth centuries, innatism—essentially, the idea that women are innately inferior to men—dominated thought in both Europe and America. The struggle for feminine freedom centers around the elaborations of this idea of innatism and the attacks on it.

The innatist view rests on real and assumed physical differ-

The Attack on the Traditional Role

ences between the sexes. Men are superior because they are straight and angular, women inferior because they are curved and rounded. Women are assumed to have a delicate nervous system requiring medical treatment—a view that can still be seen today in the readiness of some doctors to prescribe tranquilizers and other neuroleptic drugs for women. Innatists appealed to the Bible to confirm their views. One clergyman noted that the Book of Revelations proclaimed that there would be silence in heaven for the space of half an hour—surely, he argued, that was possible only in the absence of women.

On the psychological side, woman was made out to be a nonperson. In his *Commentaries,* Blackstone wrote that "the husband and wife [are] one person in law, that is, the very being or legal existence of the woman is suspended during marriage or at least is incorporated and consolidated into that of her husband. . . . For this reason a man cannot grant anything to his wife, or enter into a covenant with her; for the grant would suppose her separate existence; and to covenant with her would be only to covenant with himself" (Blackstone, 1966, p. 442). In other words, at marriage, the woman's legal standing as a person was destroyed, and she was subsumed into the legal personality of her husband.

With the Enlightenment these misogynistic theories took another form. Rousseau, in his novel *Emile,* argued that only if the woman is revered as the throne of sensuality can the sexes be equal physically; otherwise the woman, having less physical strength than the man, will be subject to a life of rape.

Surprisingly, Charles Darwin's evolutionary theories also urged the inferiority of women, especially his theory of sexual selection. In human beings, he believed, neither age, temperament, social position, nor any other factor approached the scope of the differences caused by the dissimilarity in men's and women's sexual natures. In his *Folkways,* William Sumner found sexual selection of crucial importance because the division of responsibilities between the sexes had such vast political and economic implications. In his view, specialization endowed each sex with different but complementary abilities from birth, making equality an "incongruous predicate." The human female was seen as the passive factor in the evolutionary process. Darwinists showed that while sexual selection was the prerogative of the male among higher animals, among lower animals it was the female that possessed the power of sexual selection and the male that exhibited secondary sexual characteristics to attract the female. Carl Vogt, the Geneva scholar, even felt that the woman, being closer to the animal world, provided a model for studying the link between man and ape.

Darwinian theories fueled interest in the field of eugenics. As the study of eugenics advanced, more people supported controlling the evolution of the race, the trademark of the eugenic societies. It is only recently that these arguments from evolution have been abandoned, or at least relegated to a secondary role. With the development of anthropology, it became the general belief that women's natures are determined more by their culture than by biology, although obviously the two must interact. The balance between them remains an open question. Indeed, the current vogue in the field of sociobiology is an attempt to redress what some sociobiologists consider an overemphasis on culture, even as the emphasis on culture was initially an attempt to redress the Darwinian overemphasis on biology.

In all these discussions of women, the question arose: How would the race continue if women refused to bear children? In 1916, two severe critics of feminism, Mr. and Mrs. John Martin, deplored the fact that women hungry for college degrees and self-fulfillment outside the home during their childbearing years forfeited maternity. According to them, nature implanted a strong sex urge in man in order to avoid racial extinction, but woman, with a feebler sex drive, had no such safeguard. Many eugenicists lamented the trend of declining fertility and advocated winning women over to the idea of a large family, but in this century women have, generally speaking, been reluctant to go back to the large families that were so common earlier.

The innatist argument had something to say about woman's intellectual capacities as well. According to early medieval treatises, the direct relationship between the woman's weak physique and her brain caused her very active mind, if unrestrained, to overtax her delicate nervous system by a constant demand for a rapid flow of sense data that her softer and smaller muscles could not shut down. The vogue of phrenology in the early part of the nineteenth century reinforced the belief in mental differences between the sexes and female inferiority.

Overall, the innatist consensus was that the mental powers of women were circumscribed by female reason, wit, imagination, curiosity, memory, and imitation. The widespread acceptance of a limited female mind laid the rationale for restricting woman's opportunities in society. This belief in the inability of the feminine mind to perform like the masculine mind led to separate education for the two sexes. Women themselves suggested various changes in education. Abigail Adams, wife of the second president, suggested the need for a new approach to feminine education. In a letter to her husband, John, she said she could hear of the brilliant accomplishments of her sex with pleasure but at the same time she regretted the trifling, narrow, contracted educational females of her own country" (Withey, 1981).

Even psychoanalysts have been influenced by these hoary ideas. The nineteenth century psychologist William James adhered to the theory that women mature early, men late. In 1890 he argued that the woman of twenty had a firm, intuitive grasp of life with permanent likes and dislikes; for all practical purposes she was a finished product. Freud as well, whose views on women have by and large been superseded by later knowledge, claimed that the thirty-year-old man retained youthfulness and was still choosing and developing the possibilities before him, while a woman of the same age almost frightened observers with her "psychological rigidity and unchangeability" (Freud, [1933] 1964, p. 134). It was as if she had no paths open, as if the difficult development of femininity had exhausted all the possibilities of the individual.

The common-sense "proof" of woman's innate sexual nature has always been strong, and innatists have often claimed that women's inescapable fate from the creation of Eve was to be feminine in character. According to innatists, a person had only to observe a young girl and boy to quickly perceive that they are distinctive human beings developing in different directions and with different motivations. Although innatists were unanimous in their view of woman's instinctive sexual character, two conflicting views on the value of femininity existed at the end of the eighteenth century. One group of innatists emphasized the evilness of woman's character and sternly admonished society to guard against the unwholesome influence women had on individuals and society. The other group of innatists celebrated the goodness of woman's character, noting its radiant effects on men, children, and institutions. Here is the old dichotomy between the angel and the witch, the virgin and the whore.

The latter strand of innatism, stressing woman's good character, has dominated American ideas for longer than the opposing view. It has also been responsible, at least in part, for producing the concept of the eminence of feminine conscience in human affairs. Once each year, on Mother's Day, these innatists mix a degree of sentiment, derived from their view of the inferiority of women, with the honest, sincere praise women deserve for their hard work and unselfish activities. It is this sugar-coated innatist view of the character of woman that is often highlighted in churches and at lawn parties; it is also the image of women held up to the avarege child: "Mother knows best," an image demolished by psychoanalytic research but recently revived.

A combination of old and new innatist views was presented by Helen B. Andelin in her widely read book, *Fascinating Womanhood* (1980). The primary task of every woman who wants to be truly feminine, according to Andelin, is to develop a dual nature: an angelic side to arouse in man a feeling approaching worship, and a human side to fascinate, amuse, and stimulate the masculine desire to protect and provide for her. Woman's innate nature makes it easy for her to fill this double role.

The Psychoanalytic View

Although Darwinism maintained a strong hold on American thought patterns at the turn of the century, it soon shared the limelight with psychoanalysis, which brought new dimensions to the study of woman's character. Sigmund Freud's view that Americans too strongly repress their sexual energy encouraged the younger generation to attack traditional moral standards. Freud's notion of powerful sexual drives combined with alcohol, the automobile, and sentiment to set the stage for the freedom and license of the Roaring Twenties.

The Attack on the Traditional Role

Although the writings of Freud and other leading psychoanalysts can be interpreted to show that analysts are against women's liberation, this is a gross distortion. One of Freud's major contributions to the problem of hysteria was the observation that sexual repression leads to actual physical illness. He also argued that repression fueled the demand for more sexual freedom, especially in the early years of the century. Freud was opposed to sexual repression, but he also held that the goal was not simple sexual release but the formation of a vigorous character structure that could work and love (Fine, 1990a).

On the current scene many holdovers of the innatist ideas can still be found. There are diehards who believe only in the traditional behavior of the sexes. There are others who preach a radical release of sexuality, as in the Roaring Twenties. Then there are those who vociferously deplore the fact that a woman is a woman and not a man (as in *My Fair Lady*, where Henry Higgins sings, "Why can't a woman be more like a man?"). Even the anthropologist Sara Blaffer Hardy has written a book about "the woman who never evolved," going back to the wish to change the course of evolution (Hardy, 1981).

All innatist theories have served the purpose of rationalizing the mistreatment of women through the ages. Woman is innately inferior; hence anything done to her is justified. Woman has no real mind, so do not give her an education. Woman's body is weak, so make it worse by senseless medical and pseudo-medical measures.

Suffering and disappointment have long been the lot of women. Perhaps the most graphic piece of literature on women's suffering is "The Song of the Shirt," by Thomas Hood, which first appeared in *Punch* in 1843 (Jerrold, 1980). Almost any stanza of this lament about a poor woman "plying her needle and thread" gives a fine sense of the whole:

> Work! Work! Work!
> While the cock is crowing aloof.
> And work - work - work
> Till the stars shine through the roof.
> It's oh, to be a slave
> Along with the barbarous Turk,

> Where woman has never a soul to save
> If this is Christian work.

As for the spiritual side of oppression, there is no better document in the literature than the paper by nineteenth-century suffragist Lucy Stone entitled "Disappointment Is the Lot of Woman" (Rossi, 1973, pp. 413-473). A hundred years after they were written, her words still sting:

> From the first years to which my memory stretches, I have been a disappointed woman. When, with my brothers, I reached forth after the sources of knowledge, I was reproved with: "It isn't fit for you. It doesn't belong to women." Then there was but one college in the world where women were admitted, and that was in Brazil. I would have found my way there, but by the time I was prepared to go, one was opened in the young State of Ohio—the first in the U.S., where women and Negroes could enjoy opportunities with white men. I was disappointed when I came to seek a profession worthy and immortal—every employment was closed to me, except those of the teacher, the seamstress and the housekeeper. In education, in marriage, in religion, in everything, disappointment is the lot of woman.

The Search for Equality

In a country that saw so many movements designed to remedy the plight of the poor, the needy, the homeless, and the weak, it was to be expected that women would have their turn. And indeed, since roughly the American Revolution, there has been a steady increase in the freedom that the law allows women and in the ways in which they can regulate their lives. The goal of full equality with men has not yet been reached, but certainly women have gained much greater freedom than they ever had before. This search for equality is still going on.

In the past, when husbands beat their wives, their actions were often justified by law. In recent years, campaigns have sprung up to eradicate the beating of wives. The term "battered woman" has come into popular discourse. Really, this should be a police matter, but the plain fact is that the police often turn away from

The Attack on the Traditional Role

domestic violence. The sociologist Richard Gelles (1974) has gathered extensive data on violence in the family and has shown that the family is a major locus of violence and homicide. Home strife contributes to a large proportion of the murders committed in the United States. In Detroit, labeled the "deadliest city" because its homicide rate in 1972 was the highest of any American city with a population over one million, four out of five murders involved people who knew each other—friends, neighbors, and relatives, especially the latter.

Formerly, the denigrating image of women forced them into a position where they could not enjoy their bodies. Menstruation, instead of a natural function, became a "curse," and numerous myths grew up around it. Menstruation was supposed to release a toxin, known as amenotoxin, that withered flowers and other living creatures. In many cultures, women have been segregated for periods of time to keep their menstrual poisons away from others. Even today the very orthodox Jew will not shake hands with a strange woman because she might be menstruating. Until recently, men and women were supposed to refrain from sexual intercourse during the menstrual period, since the blood was seen as contaminating.

Up until quite recently, women were forced into harmful clothes of all kinds, such as corsets, girdles, brassieres that hurt, and the like. A picture of women on the bathing beach in 1890 would make anyone laugh today, yet the camouflaging clothing was absolutely required at that time. In some sexually repressed cultures today women and men are not permitted to share the beach together. The freedom of clothing is a great boon to womankind, representing an essential step forward in the liberation of the woman's body.

Women have slowly been establishing their right to full sexual pleasure. As the Freudian theses about sexuality and illness became widely known, they were at first fought bitterly. It was not until the Masters-Johnson studies in the 1960s were published that the existence of a sexual cycle in women parallel to that of men was firmly established in professional and popular minds. The immediate response to sexual stimulation in both sexes is myotonia (muscle tension) and vasoconstriction (blood flow). Vaginal lubrication in the female was seen as the neurophysiological parallel to erection in the male as a major signal of sexual arousal. Like Kinsey, Masters and Johnson concluded that clitoral stimulation was central to female responses and demonstrated that all physiological orgasms, whether achieved by masturbation or intercourse, are physiologically similar. These studies firmly established the capacity of women for full sexual pleasure equal to that of men.

At present, the late twentieth-century sexual revolution is still in full swing, with an unknown outcome. As Myrna Lewis writes in her interesting "History of Female Sexuality in the United States" (1980), "There is much in female sexuality that is truly unique, especially physiologically, but inhibitions, stereotypes and false premises must be disposed of before this uniqueness can be fully discerned" (p. 36). In other words, the major need for both sexes today is for more and better sex education. This is especially true since the appearance of AIDS in the early 1980s because one of the methods of transmission of this fatal disease is sexual contact. Recent studies indicate, for example, that most college students are familiar with all the venereal diseases and their symptoms, including AIDS, but that many nevertheless practice sex indiscriminately.

The United States has become a fairly free country so far as women's bodies are concerned. In other cultures, such as most of Africa, women are still cruelly mistreated. An Egyptian physician, Nawal El Saadawi, has described the terrible trauma she experienced as a young girl when she was suddenly seized by two older women and forced to undergo a clitoridectomy. In the United States, clitoridectomies were performed on young girls until after World War II to prevent them from masturbating.

However, it is clear that women have yet to achieve full physical and psychological control over their own bodies. A major indicator of this is the continuing struggle over the right to abortion. It is within the memories of many living today how girls and women were forced in the past to submit to illegal abortions with the direst of consequences, including death or serious illness. Other indicators: The bulimia-anorexia combination has become very frequent among young girls; a mortality rate has even been computed for it. Commonly, women are much more depressed than men; postmenstrual and premenstrual tension are both frequent, although recently claims have been made that they have an organic compo-

The Attack on the Traditional Role 11

nent. Hysterectomies are said to be performed on women much more often than the comparable prostatectomies on men.

Attitudes towards women's intellects have been changing. For a long time, women were supposed to be innately more stupid than men, so that educational opportunities were closed to them. The alleged intellectual inferiority of women was underscored in many different ways until the intelligence tests came along to disprove the idea. Not only are women not inferior to men, they are actually superior in some ways. For example, women are generally stronger in verbal fluency and linguistics, men in science and mathematics. However, there are many exceptions to these generalizations. There is, to take just one example, the remarkable story of the three Polgar sisters, Hungarian girls who made it to the top of the chess world. Their father, a Hungarian psychologist, had originally tried to train them in mathematics, but after a short time they evinced more interest in chess. In short order, and at an exceptionally early age, they attained the master's level in chess. One of them later became the first woman ever to achieve a grand master rating.

The damage caused by innatist theories was also psychological. Many women felt the need, for emotional reasons, to be inferior to men, fearing that if they were superior, men would not want to marry them. Accordingly, they unconsciously did poorly in various subjects because their desire for marriage was stronger than their desire for academic prestige. In some women, this self-repression led to a tendency to depression. Psychoanalysts like Helene Deutsch stressed the narcissism, depression, and penis envy of women, without realizing that they were dealing with culture-bound phenomena. Later generations of psychoanalysts were quick to dispute Deutsch's theories, insisting that the sense of inadequacy foisted on women by the culture leads them to underestimate their abilities and consequently to do badly in school. Today most psychoanalysts believe that innately men and women are equal and that the differences that exist are due mainly to cultural factors and parental pressures.

In the social field, women have begun to overcome a variety of kinds of discrimination. It took centuries to realize that women could vote as intelligently as men (to the extent that men do vote intelligently—some studies indicate that in most elections some 20 percent of the electorate does not have the foggiest notion of what the election is all about). Once given the vote, women were able to move ahead toward positions of importance in the government. The first woman justice of the Supreme Court, Sandra O'Connor, was appointed by Ronald Reagan; no doubt many others will follow in the course of time. While full equality between men and women is still quite a way off, the idea is there, and once ideas take hold they have a way of persisting. As Freud once put it, the voice of reason is weak, but it persists until it gets a hearing.

Prostitution was not eliminated in the nineteenth century, but the white slavery trade did disappear, and the gaudy red-light districts that dotted every major city in the world became ever smaller and more marginal. Underground prostitution probably never will disappear, but the old tradition in which prostitutes were held in virtual slavery is not likely to come back.

One of the first blows for the liberation of modern women was struck by Mary Wollstonecraft in 1793, with the publication of her book *A Vindication of the Rights of Women*. The movement for the liberation of women has passed through many stages in different countries since then. In the United States, a landmark document was the so-called Seneca Falls declaration (Rossi, 1973, pp. 413-442), which emerged from a meeting held on July 19, 1848. As the declaration stated: "The history of mankind is a history of repeated injuries and usurpations on the part of men toward women, having its direct object the establishment of an absolute tyranny over her. To prove this, let facts be submitted to a candid world."

Other factors contributing to the sorry plight of women were given short shrift—social conditions, physical and mental illness, war, slavery, economic exploitation, and so on. In plain words, the declaration held that woman was in bad shape because of man's tyranny, and this tyranny must come to an end. The consequences of this belief for the theory and practice of psychoanalysis form the subject of the next chapter.

2 | Psychoanalysis and Women's Liberation

From the time of Mary Wollstonecraft until today, women have protested bitterly against their lot in life, tending to blame it on men more than anything else. In more recent years this attack on men has turned into an attack on psychoanalysis, which has been seen as a "male" science intended to continue the degradation of women. Anyone familiar with psychoanalysis knows that this is nonsense, but the attacks continue unchecked. It is time to correct this misconception.

Feminist writers have argued that women have been forced into an inferior position, a kind of "domestic tyranny" (Pleck, 1987a), and given little chance of getting out of it. Exactly the same general view is held by psychoanalysts. The major differences are two: First, psychoanalysts believe that men are not inherently sadistic but are made so by their environment. Second, psychoanalysis has also investigated the relationship of women with their mothers, thus revealing another potent source of their subservience and discontent.

It is true that many of the pioneers in women's liberation endured almost unimaginable suffering. As a child in England, Mary Wollstonecraft saw her mother abused by a tyrannical husband who drank too much and squandered what little money the family had. Later she helped a sister escape from a similarly cruel husband. She herself attempted suicide when a man with whom she had an affair left her immediately following the birth of their child. She died of complications following childbirth, at the age of thirty-eight.

However, this is only half of the story. What was the lot of men during this period? Slavery, also known as serfdom, existed in many countries around the world. Men were drafted into the army and forced, whether they liked it or not, to shoot other men. Men who worked for a living were often little more than wage slaves, living a miserable life and dying an early death.

Modern man is only somewhat better off. A typical case history of a modern man might read as follows: John was a civil service worker who became ill at an early age with stomach ulcers, which severely restricted his diet and other activities. The area he enjoyed most was his work, and in thirty-five years he rarely missed a day. With his wife and two children he had little contact, especially when he started to work at night. His only concern about his daughter was when she decided to move in with her boyfriend without getting married first. This aroused his indignation, and he insisted that she marry, which she did. When his son left home at eighteen to seek his fortune in another part of the country, John said nothing. In this way he lived out his life.

In other words, the notion of blighted female lives can only be properly understood when compared with blighted male lives. Blighted lives are blighted, regardless of gender.

The Attack on Motherhood

While it was easy for women to blame men, and for men to blame women, the real trouble lies in the larger social system. Betty Friedan's development is a case in point. When she published *The Feminine Mystique* in 1963, she was struggling to free herself from fifteen years as a suburban housewife, years that featured three children and a failed marriage. Her own salvation was wrapped up in dismissing homemaking as comprising "tasks for feeble-minded girls and eight-year-olds," and it was to be twenty years before she could look motherhood in the eye again. In her 1981 book, *The Second Stage,* she acknowledges the central role of children and family in women's lives. Thus she was able to say that the failure of the women's movement was its blind spot about the family.

In her significant book *A Lesser Life,* Sylvia Hewlett makes the important point that motherhood is the problem that modern

Psychoanalysis and Women's Liberation

feminists cannot face. Her main thesis is that American women have stressed most strongly the need for economic equality, but at the cost of losing love, marriage, and motherhood, and in the end not even getting economic equality.

In her chapter on motherhood, she argues that motherhood is not going out of style. In 1980, only 10 percent of all women aged forty to forty-four were childless. The only exceptions to this trend are elite professional women. A large proportion of these are single or divorced, and a significant proportion remain childless. Census figures show that 20 percent of all highly educated women (women with graduate training) remain childless.

Hewlett goes on to say that the feminists of the modern women's movement made one gigantic mistake: They assumed that modern women wanted nothing to do with children. As a result, they have consistently failed to incorporate the bearing and rearing of children into their vision of a "liberated" life. This mistake has had serious repercussions.

Admittedly, bringing up a child is no easy task. Babies cry and scream, they throw up, they become ill, they do not sleep too well (especially in the beginning), they may cry incessantly, they have to be watched to avoid serious accidents (which occur anyhow). Yet women throughout the ages have accepted these tasks, more or less readily, because of the compensatory satisfaction derived from bringing up a healthy, active, constructive child.

As Hewlett points out, the radical feminists went over to a vigorous attack on motherhood and its alleged benefits. The titles of their books are illustrative: Jill Johnston's *Lesbian Nation*, which declares that heterosexuality is the female form of treason; Germaine Greer's *The Female Eunuch*, which finds an explanation for impotence in being female; Kate Millett's *Sexual Politics*, in which the person becomes political and sex is redefined as a power struggle; Katherine Perutz's *Marriage Is Hell*, which argues that marriage is precisely that; and Ellen Peck's *The Baby Trap*, which reveals how and why babies are incompatible with liberation. The slogans of the 1960s and 1970s were extraordinary: marriage is hell, sex is political, coitus is killing, married women are prostitutes, babies are traps, intercourse is rape, love is slavery, families are prisons, and men are enemies.

Whether American women are truly missing out on marriage, as Hewlett contends, is still an open question. Considerable debate on this point was generated in the late 1980s by an unsettling report on educated women's marriage probabilities. This "study"—in fact, only a few paragraphs in a 5,000-word paper—was greeted with skepticism among sociologists and demographers (Hewlett, 1986).

Now, because the authors, in response to colleagues' suggestions, have eliminated the category of "college-educated white women" from their calculations, and because they are using more recent demographic data than they had in 1986, it is virtually impossible to recalculate the marriage-probability statistics using the revised model.

Only one figure in the revised paper is remotely relevant to the figures that gained worldwide attention. In the 1986 draft, it was estimated that 22 percent of white female college graduates born in the years 1953 to 1957 would never marry. In the revised study, it is estimated that 11.5 percent of white women with more than a high school education who were born in the early 1950s will never marry.

Thus we are led back to the truism that there are three kinds of liars—liars, damned liars, and statistics. The question of whether advanced education would hurt a woman's chances to marry has always plagued women who wanted higher education but has never received a clear-cut answer. A lot depends on how men react to women's advanced education, which in turn depends just as much on their own self-esteem as on their estimate of what makes for a successful life.

The young woman today who does not desire an early marriage risks postponing marriage until it is too late for childbearing. In analysis this conflict is handled in terms of the childhood background of the woman; generalizations are inadequate.

A typical case is that of Felicia, a young woman who married right after high school. In quick succession she had two children, then discovered that her husband was a severe bore. Eventually, she divorced him to enter a new career in business but found that bringing up two children with inadequate support from her husband was a great handicap.

Ideally, when a boy and girl start going steady at an early age (fifteen or sixteen) and it eventuates in marriage, the best outcome is a situation that does allow each to pursue his or her own career. Usually, for this to work out, the parents have to be sympathetic to the arrangement, which is not always the case. Thus, in practice, whatever the theories of women's liberation may be, the practicalities of love and marriage and children tend to be the weightiest factors in life decisions.

Many prominent figures in the women's movement have publicized their own personal solutions to the dilemmas of motherhood and marriage. Betty Friedan left her husband and children to devote all her time to the movement, but later became disillusioned. Others, too, have devoted themselves to the movement at the cost of some personal happiness. Gloria Steinem's mother gave up her career to help her father, a move that Steinem did not care to emulate. Steinem's mother also suffered a bout of mental illness that followed years of trying to take care of her baby and be the wife of a kind but financially irresponsible man. In Steinem's autobiography, not one word is devoted to motherhood, family, or children, as though she had put all these crucial questions completely out of mind.

Thus, whatever theoretical solution is offered to the problem of the woman's life, motherhood remains one of her major concerns. To go through life without a child is still a painful way out for most women. It is also a painful way out for most men (Fine, 1989).

Safeguarding Motherhood

One of the primary difficulties of motherhood is that safeguards have to be built around it, to ensure the maximum benefit to both mother and child. First of all, there are physical dangers connected with bearing children; not all mothers survive it. It is only in the twentieth century that medicine has learned enough about the birthing process to be able to intervene effectively. Prior to that, some limitations had to be placed on the woman as well as on the man. Even today, when so much more is known, some limitations are still necessary.

Obviously, motherhood involves more than just giving birth. It leads to a whole complex of feelings and emotions that are vital to the human race. The mother has been glorified as the "angel in the house," the source of all love, goodness, and caring, the person who makes the greatest difference in the development of mankind. Indeed, for centuries it was widely believed that originally all societies were organized around the mother, as in many animal species, and that the father was only incidental. This notion has been dispelled only because of direct observations of many different societies by anthropologists working in the field.

The structure of the family reflects the need to safeguard the health and welfare of the mother. The traditional nuclear family did this by providing a known and secure role for all the people in the family—father, mother, and children. The clash between feminism and psychoanalysis, when it exists, and it often does exist, lies in the realistic need to make provisions for adequate mothering.

Psychoanalysis did not hit upon the central importance of mothering in human existence right away; as a matter of fact, it only came to light fully after Freud's death in 1939. It was only after R. Spitz (1966), drawing on research done before World War II, showed how much pathology could result from maternal inadequacy that there was a full recognition of the significance of the mother-child bond. In his massive three-volume work, *Attachment and Loss*, John Bowlby summarized the voluminous literature on the vicissitudes of the early mother-child relationship. Bowlby's work was originally carried out at the request of the United Nations, thus emphasizing the universal relevance of analytic ideas. (Bowlby's ideas will be examined in more depth in Chapter Seven.)

Today it is generally recognized that special measures are needed to safeguard the mothering process. Maternity leave, special home care, breast feeding, guaranteed income for mothers, and the like are only some of the measures that have been developed or promoted to make sure that the mothering process proceeds optimally.

In addition, the importance of the father in the early life of the child is now fully recognized. As a result, the emphasis has shifted from the mother to the father to the total family structure. This process is typical of the thinking about children. Where before, as a result of anthropological evidence and psychoanalytic research, the child was seen to be largely dependent on the mother for warmth, attention, and love, now it is seen that it is the whole family system that is at stake. The work of psychologist R. P. Rohner (1975) showing that parental acceptance and rejection are the primary variables in the self-esteem of the child is particularly relevant.

Roots of Feminism in Childhood

A major difference between the women's liberation movement and psychoanalysis is that women's liberation deals in behavioristic terms, while psychoanalysis deals in inner-psychological terms. Thus, for many decades, the women's movement was focused on getting women the vote; once the vote was obtained, it was realized that nothing much had changed. In psychoanalysis, on the other hand, the procedure is geared toward making the woman happier inside without ignoring the external circumstances. To change behavior or society is good, according to psychoanalytic theory, but if it is not going to change the inner-psychological balance to help the woman enjoy life more, it is going to be of little individual value. Thus, one change after another has been introduced in women's lives, yet the same complaints persist uninterrupted—chiefly the complaint that men reduce women to second-class citizens.

Most criticism of psychoanalysis is incredibly misguided since it takes the theoretical positions out of context and makes a mockery of them, or turns them into a philosophical argument. Here are two typical instances of women in therapy whose feelings about women's liberation came from their childhood and who worked out these feelings in different ways.

Susan was a thirty-year-old social worker who was almost rabidly in favor of women's liberation. All her troubles came from being a woman; if she were a man, life would be entirely different. Her favorite fantasy was that some day she could chuck her job and travel around Europe, tasting whatever pleasures she could find (including sexual) wherever she could find them.

Susan's childhood was marked by the fact that her parents' marriage was extremely unhappy. Her father had at one time been an actor, then, unable to make it in that field, had switched to driving a garbage truck. Of this he was terribly ashamed, as was his wife, and it was not permitted for anyone in the family to mention it publicly.

Except for the blindness of their feelings about one another, Susan's family led an uneventful life. This "uneventfulness" was in itself the most salient feature of her home life. Her parents simply did not interact; her father went his way, her mother went hers. Susan's father spent much of his time bewailing his glorious past; her mother, who was slightly deaf, kept pretty much to herself.

In college Susan joined a women's consciousness-raising group. Two of the members of this group were overt lesbians. Susan was envious of them, not critical, although she felt herself to be completely heterosexual.

Eventually, almost in spite of herself, Susan married and had two children. The marriage was a devitalized one, though without overt conflict. As the children grew up, Susan held onto her fantasy of being single and traveling all over Europe. She bewailed her fate but could see no way out. Her sexual feelings only came to the fore when her older son reached puberty and started talking more about sex.

For Susan, belief in women's liberation served the purpose of expressing her wish for greater freedom and meaning in her life. It came out in terms of her feelings about her femininity because that was the accepted form in her circle. Eventually analysis convinced Susan that there was more to life than regretting her gender identity.

Like Susan, Rosa was the daughter of two people who were very unhappy together. Her mother, the daughter of a wealthy family, had not been able to marry until late in life, at which time she picked an aspiring young artist who was only too happy to have a wealthy woman sponsor him in his artistic career, which had bogged down. He was also a womanizer who did not consider that marriage should interfere with his womanizing. At parties he would openly make a play for any attractive woman. His wife was angry about this but said nothing. (See Chapter Four for a discussion of Rosa's mother, Karen.)

The couple had two children, a boy and a girl. The boy, a favorite of both, did well, with a good marriage and success in his

Psychoanalysis and Women's Liberation

chosen profession of college teaching. Rosa, however, had numerous problems. Throughout high school and college she was passionately attached to a girlfriend, who later became a psychotherapist after first spending several years as an interior designer. Rosa often wondered why she and her friend had never engaged in any physical sex play.

Rosa was more identified with her father than with her mother. Throughout childhood she preferred boys' clothes, boys' games, and boys' toys. This male identification was so strong that she literally believed that at puberty she would grow a penis. When this did not happen, and she menstruated instead, she cried all day.

Although outwardly heterosexual, dating boys and going to parties, inwardly Rosa felt more homosexual, though without ideas of physical intimacy. Her identification with her father led her into an artistic field in which she did well. It was understandable that with such a background Rosa would become a passionate feminist. Yet she retained enough identification with mother to want marriage too. Her first marriage was a poor one, to an asexual, domineering businessman. After many bitter fights they broke up. She then became quite pessimistic about her chances of finding another man, and eventually she made plans to leave the city. At the last minute, however, she ran into an old acquaintance who renewed his interest in her, and she stayed.

In Rosa's case, the contradictory identifications with her mother and father explained her ambivalent feelings about being a woman and about the women's liberation movement. Toward her own child, a daughter, she developed a strong affection that helped to carry her through the vicissitudes of living.

Men's Attitudes Toward Women's Liberation

In the light of Susan and Rosa's personal struggles to come to terms with the women's liberation movement, it is interesting to look at the varied reactions "women's lib" arouses in men. In Shere Hite's book on female sexuality (1983) is this comment by a man who admits to feeling "threatened" by the movement: "I think this women's lib is a good thing. But it is going too fast for most men to adjust to. It becomes very confusing at times because it is so hard to understand a woman's way of thinking. They want to be free and liberated, but they also want to be protected and taken care of. I see many of my friends' marriages going down the drain because of the jobs their wives have" (p. 302). Rather revealingly, this man later added, in reference to his own job, "Personally, I feel like a drone bee in a giant beehive."

Other men were angry that women seemed to be getting the best of both worlds. As one man said (p. 303), "I'm all for real equality, but I think women want to eliminate their disadvantages and keep their special privileges and morally superior attitude. . . . Like passive compliance and desireless seduction, 'liberation' now means that the average woman believes it is her right to change things she believes to be to her benefit."

Many men who said they were basically in favor of women's liberation also said they were angry at "loud" or "militant" women, women who were the opposite of "supportive" and "loving." Thus, one man said (p. 304), "I think that women today are saying that they should be considered as human beings, with the same desires and capabilities that men have. I agree. I am glad that such things have been pointed out to me. From time to time I regress and appreciate gentle reminders. But militant women merely antagonize me. I think these women are bitchy to begin with. If they would not be bitchy about women's lib, they would be bitchy about something else."

Many men were confused about the meaning of the women's movement and gave contradictory answers. One man said (p. 208), "I hate women who don't recognize the differences between men and women. I hate women who in the name of former repression are exclusionary and even more repressive than any man I know ever was. . . . But I like strong women. I like tall women. I like women with stamina. I dislike women who play on the weak side of their femininity. I dislike 'dumb blondes.' I dislike women who curse worse than sailors. I dislike women who want to be men and always dress as men. Women contribute motherhood, vast intelligence, the softening of civilization. . . . Yet I don't see woman as chattel or less and inferior. I see them as superior and important. I do believe we must protect motherhood."

A few men actually insisted there is no oppression of women

in society; individual women are themselves to blame. One said (p. 310), "Liberation from what? I never knew they were enslaved." Another man even claimed withdrawal from the problem (p. 311): "I don't think about it. It is a problem women must resolve. It has no effect on men." In fact, when asked, "What do you think about women's liberation? How has it affected your relationships?" most men said, "Not at all."

All in all, there can be no doubt that the movement to liberate women has had both positive and negative effects on men and women. On the positive side, it has increased the self-esteem of women, opened the way for entrance into many professions and business opportunities, improved women's sex lives, and led to a better approach to life's rewards. On the negative side, it has tended to increase women's anger at men and at times, paradoxically, has made women even more bitter about their lot. Part of this frustration derives from the inability to equalize or overcome the biological hurdles nature has imposed on them. Any special arrangements made by society seem to produce problems in the contrary direction; that is, if women are favored too much, men feel put down.

In one area, however, there is almost unanimous agreement. The public has finally been made aware of the seriousness of the problem of violence against women, and it has in general reacted with indignation and cries for improvement. In one sense this is a worldwide trend. The beginning of this century saw incredible episodes of wholesale massacres, wars, genocide, and the extermination of millions of innocents. Women have suffered from these hatreds even more than men, although numbers alone hardly tell the tale.

Thus, whatever society does, the problem remains. The psychoanalytic solution is to pursue the analytic ideal for both sexes, and perhaps in the wake of the world revolution that now seems to be going on this may well be an ever more plausible way out.

3 | Love

It is the general opinion that love is more important to a woman than to a man, and many writers have taken the position that women's troubles are due to frustrated love, men's to frustrated sexuality. Byron put the basic thought in words almost 200 years ago: "Man's love is of man's life a thing apart, / 'Tis woman's whole existence" (Byron, [1819] 1984). Yet even though he praised women for their capacity to love (as have many others), Byron was perceptive enough to say as well: "Sweet is revenge—especially to women."

Love and sexuality are very close; in fact, it is virtually impossible to separate the two, though essential to try. In this chapter we shall focus on love, in the next on sexuality.

Understanding of any woman's life can begin with her love life. Most striking in this love life are the high spots of intense and deep romance, of love in the ordinary sense of the word, love between a man and a woman. Yet closer examination reveals, as Freud pointed out, that the intense raptures of love depend very strongly on the whole history of the woman; in other words, love develops, it does not come to life full-blown. People like to think that love's raptures explode as if by one magical push, yet more careful study shows that love has a long history. This fact in a sense defines the process of the analysis of love in the therapeutic situation: women come to therapy because they find love a source of suffering rather than joy, and it is up to the analyst to explain where this suffering comes from so that they can get over it. It is not uncommon for a woman to become depressed (sometimes to the point of suicide) because she is so frustrated in love, and such a depression can only be understood—and overcome—in terms of an analysis of the woman's whole life.

Most women come to grief on the problems of loving. The woman who is rejected by her lover usually does not realize that the roots of her suffering go all the way back to her childhood, especially to her relationship with her father and mother. In fact, all the interpersonal relationships of the woman throughout her life go back to this early relationship with her parents. This is why psychologists have focused so strongly on the earliest years; our experience confirms Freud's position that the hysteric suffers primarily from reminiscences.

In this chapter and the next few, I propose to take some typical forms of love suffering and show how they conform to a pattern that can be traced throughout a person's life history.

Early Childhood Relationships

For girls as well as boys, the first relationship in life is always with the mother. For the young infant, the mother is either accepting or rejecting, and this dichotomy of acceptance-rejection has become the focus of all research on infancy and the mother-child relationship (Rohner, 1975).

From the mother the girl turns to the father. How she turns to him depends very strongly on the relationship with the mother. If the relationship is normal and positive, she turns to the father with longing and love—identifying with a loving mother all the way. If, however, the relationship with the mother is stormy and conflictual (which is usually the case), she turns to the father as to a savior.

Rohner, an anthropological psychologist who has studied parental acceptance and rejection in depth, found that the effects of maternal rejection are universal and harmful. He wrote that "rejected children throughout the world, as compared with accepted children, are significantly more hostile-expressive (or passive-aggressive). These children also tend to devaluate themselves, to be uncomfortable with themselves, and to perceive themselves as being worthless or worthy only of condemnation. Moreover, rejected children are often more dependent than accepted children; they are more clingy and attention seeking than accepted children" (pp. 100-101).

From these early experiences, the child's love develops and moves in various directions. It is an accepted principle that the child who is loved will love in turn. Thus, love in the earliest years has been identified as the child's most significant experience.

However, while the popular myth has it that all parents are wonderful and loving, the clinical realities are entirely different. Many mothers mistreat their children in awful ways, which are detailed in the many case histories that appear in technical and popular journals. In fact, the "abused child" who requires protection from his or her parents has become the common coin of all popular histories. In addition, the Oedipus complex, or the need to love one parent rather than the other, enters in. Freud considered the Oedipus complex to be the common root of all neuroses (and psychoses), which is an exaggeration. But the feelings involved in the Oedipus complex—the boy's love for his mother, the girl's for her father—enter into any extended discussion of the origins of personality. The women's liberation movement has tended to downplay this complex, focusing instead on the mother's trying to handle too many tasks early in the child's life, but the consequences for the child are similar. Certainly it is wise to simplify the mother's life as much as possible, but the psychological factors making up the Oedipal frustration will surface nonetheless.

In one case a child was brought into the hospital complaining of stomach pains. Nothing organic was found, and she was referred to psychologists. There it was ascertained that the mother was a complete paranoid schizophrenic. She had come to the United States from Poland in 1946 and developed the delusion that she was a secret agent of the Polish underground and that Hitler's agents were here trying to poison her. At times she would withhold food for two or three days from the children, convinced that agents had left poisons for them. The little girl was asked whether she really had stomachaches or whether she simply said so to please her mother. She admitted that she was doing it to please her. After the mother was hospitalized, the symptoms cleared up.

Many times a pointless love in adolescence will follow from early experiences. Cora came to treatment after a suicide attempt.

Love

She was then twenty-three, the third of four children in a solid family. Her mother was a very good mother, devoting herself to the four children and the household. Her father was a successful businessman whose major weakness was that he always demanded an impossible amount of love from each child. For example, before they went to bed he would say, "Whom do you love more, mother or father?" They knew that if they answered "mother," he would get angry, so they usually said "father," not really meaning it.

Cora was known as the life of the family; she was bright, vivacious, social, attractive. However, when still quite a young child, she developed leukemia, which eventually killed her. Unable to cope with the disease, she went steadily downhill.

In her love life, she had a boyfriend at fifteen whom she was planning to marry. His family advised him against marriage to her because she was so sick, so he broke it off, devastating her further.

When the time came for her to graduate and move out into the world, Cora was frightened by her prospects. Her relationship with her parents proved a hindrance rather than a help. Her early attachment to her mother had left Cora feeling helpless and dependent, and her father's demand that she should prefer him to her mother was also more than she could handle. She remained a dependent child, clinging to her mother and father all her life.

An entirely different pattern was seen in the case of Daisy, who came to therapy when the man with whom she had been in love suddenly abandoned her. Even during the affair with him, he had been very difficult. He was a surgeon, and often when she called him she would be told he was in surgery, where he could not be disturbed. She never knew whether this was true or an alibi.

Daisy was the older of two sisters. The family was always in bad shape, stifled by what the sociologist Cuber has called "platitudinous reassurance." Her relationship with her mother was always bad, and she had attached herself to her father from an early age.

Daisy's father was much older than her mother; it was also his second marriage. Daisy's mother was often openly contemptuous of him, insinuating that he was sexually impotent ("not much of a man"). Her consciously espoused philosophy regarding men was: "Get them for what you can get, then get rid of them."

Daisy was not in agreement with this philosophy. Instead, she sought loving and warmth rather than exploitation. When her mother married for the second time, she insisted that it was merely because her mother did not want to work; she had no love for the new man. According to Daisy, her mother demanded a life insurance policy and $40,000 in cash. (She got the policy but no cash, yet she stayed in the marriage.)

Daisy was attached to her father, and when her mother left him, she spent about a year taking care of him. In this period Daisy's father made several very seductive overtures toward her, but she did not respond.

Her life showed many ups and downs in all areas. She went to school on and off but repeatedly flunked out; in five years' time she accumulated credit for only about one year of schoolwork. In work she found that she had secretarial and accounting skills, but she could not hold a job for long. Depression would set in fairly soon, and she would quit, only to do the same thing on another job.

At nineteen she fell in love with Herman, an unemployed actor with whom she had her first extended sexual relationship. Herman turned out to have a very difficult sexual problem—he was unable to ejaculate. Clearly, he was a reminder of the impotant father. Herman told her his inability to ejaculate was her fault, a story she accepted, setting a pattern of blaming herself for the man's problems that she was to repeat many times. With her help, Herman was occasionally able to ejaculate, and eventually Daisy became pregnant and had an abortion without his knowledge. She supported both of them by working as a waitress since he wanted to leave himself free for a call from the theater. But nothing ever clicked for him.

After several months, Herman began to hit Daisy, blaming her more and more for his difficulties. This was the final straw. The relationship had begun in July, and they had married shortly thereafter. In November she left him, and in January the marriage was annulled. The whole episode, which later filled her with a deep sense of shame, was concealed from everybody, including her family.

After the breakup with Herman there followed a long series of affairs. Except for one, which culminated in engagement to a man named Juan, none of these relationships clicked. Each time she would blame herself for the man's sexual difficulties, and each time the relationship would break up.

In analysis, Daisy was able to get in touch with herself through her sexual fantasies. There were two repetitive fantasies of sudden sex that were clearly outgrowths of her longing for her father. In one she is sitting in the subway, spots a handsome man, gives him a sign that she is willing, and they go off to have sex together. In the other, she is sitting in the movies and a man sits down next to her and gradually masturbates her to orgasm.

These revelations were used first to clarify her image of herself as an abandoned woman. What was bothering her underneath was her sexually promiscuous wishes; the battle was really between her desires and her superego (internalized parents). She was jealous of Juan, partly because of her wish to have a lot of men, which she projected onto him. Eventually it became clear to her that she had subordinated her own needs to those of her husband and father because of the deep conviction that she did not deserve anything better (superego punishment). As this self-depreciation was worked out, the need to idealize a man and fall in love with him diminished. Eventually she was able to develop a more normal image of love as mutual enjoyment and fulfillment, make a happy marriage, and lead a more constructive life.

These two cases bring out a number of features of love as we see it in the clinical situation. Cora had a deep feeling of dependency on her mother, which was then transferred to the father-husband. She became fixated on her second husband and never developed herself any further. Daisy, on the other hand, was able to outgrow her mother and father and live a really adult life after a number of forays in the direction of inadequate father-substitutes.

In childhood, the little girl either hates her mother or loves her. Either way, because of the growth process, she moves on to her father. If she hates her mother, the move to her father is more exciting and she can "fall in love." This love feeling for the father then has to be outgrown; if it is not, the woman bogs down in other conflicts of childhood and suffers accordingly.

Rather than go on to cite more case histories, I would like to move the discussion to the more general question of the role of love in our society and in other societies. For while love seems to be a private feeling, a closer examination reveals that it is invariably subject to a variety of social controls. For love, in the romantic sense, threatens the social order in a number of ways, and so in most of the world love has not been given much institutional support and has been kept under strong controls (Goode, 1982). The meaning of love varies with the overall culture; its fullest flowering can only be expected to occur in a love culture.

Since the individual is so constrained to conform to his or her culture, the detachment and objectivity that would allow that person to see the culture from a different point of view are extremely difficult to achieve. Instead, there is in virtually all cultures either conformity or rebellion, neither of which leads to real love.

Individual patients in therapy cannot be expected to derive much benefit from the fact that ours is a hate culture and has been a hate culture for thousands of years. However, they can realize that love feelings and the disappointments that invariably accompany them are related in some ways to the problems that are so abundant in society, and in particular to the battles and unhappiness that existed in their families in childhood.

Intentional Love Cultures

From time immemorial, human beings, disheartened by the victory of evil in the world, have tried to withdraw into groups of their own where they could practice love and harmony, far from the madding crowd. These communitarian groups have been called intentional love cultures, since whatever their basic philosophy might be, sooner or later it turns out that they are seeking to establish a rule of love. Some of these groups have combined love with free sexuality; others have forbidden all sexuality.

According to Zablocki (1980), a new commune has been formed in the United States at least once every year for the past 300 years. Although the original ideology may vary widely, upon closer examination it turns out that the commune sample is nearly unanimous in its high regard for only one value: loving. Half the respondents rank loving as their first or second most important instrumental value, and 90 percent place it in the top half of their lists of values. "Truly it can be said that love is the common coin of the entire communitarian movement" (p. 196).

What Zablocki found is that when group members like one another, the group stays together; but if there is too much of a demand for intimacy, the group begins to fall apart. Both of these propositions are contradicted if there is a strong, charismatic leader; then whatever the leader says becomes the law.

The question of who goes into communes, or intentional love cultures, has been extensively investigated. The description given by William James almost a century ago ([1902], 1980) is still largely valid. He felt that psychologically immature individuals who were introverted and pessimistic, with a negative outlook on the world, were the ones most likely to undergo a conversion to an unorthodox religious group. He coined the terms "once-born" and "twice-born." Those who convert to a new religion or enter a commune are twice-born—they feel a tremendous uplift after wallowing for a shorter or longer period of time in a quagmire of depression, shiftlessness, and drifting. They have a new family, they have a new goal, they have a new set of values that makes them feel twice-born.

What James did not describe, but what has been described by many researchers since, is the fact that the resurgent feelings of confidence, optimism, and trust do not last indefinitely. "A great many of them begin life full of hope and enthusiasm, only to perish before being able to celebrate a first birthday" (Zablocki, 1980, p. 146). Half of the communes in his sample had disintegrated in a little over two years, and almost half of those remaining were gone after four years. However, this is not the entire picture. Some of the communes re-formed and led longer lives. But even within these re-formed communes, love for individuals was suspect. As in Aldous Huxley's 1932 caricature of communism, *Brave New World*, anyone who falls in love is suspect and often kicked out of the commune.

Judy was a typical product of the sense of aimlessness and anomie in modern society. In her despair, she joined a commune dominated by an ex-addict. Every move of hers was now prescribed. She was told when to date, when to have sexual intercourse, how to find amusement, with whom to socialize, and the like.

Then she fell in love with a new man. When she confessed this to the leader, he flew into a rage and literally kicked her downstairs. Then he expelled her from the group and forbade any member of the group to socialize with her.

A much more dramatic example of the power of the leader came out in a group that hit the headlines for a short time in the late 1970s and early 1980s. Led by the Reverend Jim Jones, 1,200 Americans, the majority of them women, emigrated to Guyana, leaving all their belongings behind in the United States. There they set up an isolated community over which Jones had complete control. Among other matters, Jones was the only one permitted to have sex (Yee and Layton, 1982). After receiving complaints from some of his constituents about the kidnapping or brainwashing of their family members, Congressman Leo Ryan left for Guyana to look at the situation firsthand. He was shot to death after his arrival at the commune. Then, at Jones's command, 908 members of the community committed suicide by drinking poison. Jones shot himself crying, "Mother, mother, please" (p. 285). Later investigation showed that almost all had committed suicide voluntarily.

The members of this community all insisted that they loved Jones, yet the outcome for many was death. Evidently, the need to obey the strong leader was the strongest motive of all.

Although the small communes that Zablocki and others investigated are made up for the most part of individuals rebelling against an ungratifying society—that is, an unloving family background—it is striking how the composition of the commune becomes increasingly similar to the pattern of the family. When group members like one another, it becomes a *happy family* (the term is used quite often), but when dyads form with too much intimacy, it becomes incestuous, arousing the same kinds of jealousies and resentments in the others that the pairing off of father and mother arouses in the average child. And overall, if the communal "father" is a powerful figure (less often the "mother"), then the previous attitudes are subordinated to the imperative to bow to the will of the leader.

Love for most people means intimacy, sexuality, and warmth. However, in the communes these feelings are forced onto the group rather than onto individual contacts. For example, one of the songs of the Oneida Community, a strong commune of the nineteenth century, went as follows:

Love

> We have built us a dome
> On one beautiful plantation
> And we all have one home
> And one family relation

In a later verse a man sings, looking at a woman near him:

> I love you, oh my sister
> But the love of God is better
> Yes the love of God is better
> Oh the love of God is best

To this she replies in kind, substituting the words "oh my brother" for "oh my sister" (pp. 249-250).

In sum, there have been innumerable intentional love cultures set up throughout history. These cultures thrive if the members love one another, but fall apart when the love becomes too intense. And overriding both considerations is the powerful influence of a charismatic father figure (on occasion a mother figure) who demands and receives absolute obedience no matter how arbitrary or irrational the demands may be.

Rebellion Against the Family

To return to our clinical discussion: The relationship between the individual love experience and the group is expressed most often in terms of the child's rebellion against her family. The following case is typical.

Frieda was the only child of two wealthy parents both of whom had inherited their money. At about the age of thirty, the father had become sick with heart and blood pressure problems, and he remained chronically worried about his condition until his death at sixty-seven. In the meantime, he would alternately remake his will or announce that he was better, both with an eye to getting Frieda's sympathy.

The mother's money came from her father, who was the patriarch of the family. He had come from Europe, impoverished, and had built up a fortune in the restaurant business. All his children participated in this business.

Frieda came to adolescence in the turbulent years of World War II. She joined the USO, like other girls of her generation, and went there almost nightly. She began to have sex indiscriminately with soldiers sometimes on her own doorstep. This behavior did not escape her mother's sharp eye, and there were continual bitter fights between mother and daughter.

After this stormy adolescence, Frieda fell in love with a dancer who was performing at a country resort where she was staying at the time. Her family objected strenuously, saying that he was an adventurer, simply interested in her money, but all to no avail.

In the meantime, the grandfather who was the family patriarch developed cancer. He blamed his granddaughter and her "loose" ways, which had shocked him, for his illness, and the family agreed with him—it was her promiscuity that had led to her grandfather's cancer. Frieda, too, accepted the verdict and felt terribly guilty about her behavior; however, this did not change anything.

In her dilemma, Frieda responded with a psychosomatic symptom—colitis (constant diarrhea). Although it made her miserable, and although her grandfather threatened to disinherit her, she went ahead with marriage to the dancer anyway.

Five years and two children later, Frieda woke up to find that she no longer loved the dancer. Moreover, she realized that the whole affair was a rationalization of her defiance. She tried to arrange a divorce, only to discover to her horror that her husband was blackmailing her; he wanted part of her grandfather's money. Her father managed to eke out a compromise, but Frieda's husband walked off with a considerable sum of money.

What happened then was another piece of rebellion. For her chores around town, Frieda had hired a car service with a very handsome chauffeur. Again she fell in love. Again the family objected, but this time she did not act prematurely. She entered analysis.

In the analysis, she discovered what all her "loves" were about. Even at that stage, her father still used to tease her unmercifully. He supported her in full, but each month he would bargain her down a little on her monetary needs, even though he was extraordinarily wealthy. Eventually, through the analysis, she was able to make a sensible marriage with a man who was her equal, found a newer, more mature kind of love, and led a more normal life than ever before.

Contradictory Aspects of Love

While love is most of all an exhilarating experience, sometimes it is also quite disturbing. A case in point is Gloria, the older of two children, who was extremely promiscuous. With none of her lovers did she expect anything permanent. Then came an affair with a man called Richard—and she fell in love.

This love upset Gloria more than any of the casual sex flings, partly because she was already married with a small child. As a result, she came to analysis. In analysis, of course, her feelings about her parents came out. Gloria's mother was a rather cold, heartless woman who at sixty was still going to dance halls to pick up younger men.

Gloria's childhood was very unhappy. Her parents had divorced when she was only three or four. One of her outstanding memories was the day that her father, who had been away from home, returned and kidnapped her younger brother. She felt terribly rejected that he had not kidnapped her. Gloria could pinpoint this event because it happened on the day World War II ended. She was four years old.

Marriage came early to Gloria, when she was still in her teens. She married a man somewhat like herself who had numerous affairs that he did not even bother to conceal from her. Since both parties had open affairs, the marriage was what we could call today an open marriage, although the term did not exist in the 1950s.

Her husband suffered from painful headaches, for which he went to psychotherapy for a number of years. Though these cleared up, the open sexuality continued for both.

Gloria, in identification with her mother, was motivated by a strong wish for revenge against men. At one time, one of her lovers called, pleading for sex on the grounds that his wife was pregnant and would not have sex with him any longer. She had sex with him while her husband was away, but when he called the next time, she put him off with an excuse. This continued for quite a while.

With her therapist, Gloria was often seductive. One time when the therapist came into the waiting room she was taking off her pantyhose; when he inquired what she was doing, she merely said she was too hot and was making herself more comfortable.

Gloria's motto had always been: "Look ma, no hands." She wanted no permanent attachments, in imitation of her mother's lifelong infidelities. That was why her sudden love for Richard was so disturbing. Her hands were on this time.

One time Richard took her to the apartment of a friend of his; while there, he took her into the bedroom and made love to her within earshot of friends, though they could not see what was going on. Gloria felt so embarrassed that when she got home she attempted suicide. It seemed to be a serious suicide attempt, though she was rather casual about the whole thing, not even bothering to put in an emergency call to her therapist. The suicide attempt passed without any sequelae.

Eventually, Gloria became pregnant, at which point she revealed to the therapist that she had lied about her age, making herself two years younger than she really was.

As this example indicates, love is not always the straightforward emotion that people think it is; unconscious and sociocultural factors play a significant role in what the person will feel. Love may cover up hatred, it may be a form of teasing, it may be a form of compliance, or it may have a variety of other meanings depending on the background of the individual. Quite characteristic of love on the current scene is its extreme changeability, especially in adolescence; love turns to hatred with astonishing rapidity.

No problems are more common in psychotherapy than those connected with love. Women come in because they feel that their husbands do not love them, or they feel unloved by their children. Most often the woman feels unloved by someone close and important—parents, even siblings and children, sometimes nowadays grandchildren.

There are two kinds of love: the romantic and the normal. The romantic arises from a background of frustration and longing. The normal arises from growing up in a healthy, normal family.

Love

Because the normal family is acutally so rare in history, and especially in our society, discussions of love are universal. Poetry and song always deal with love, and the average woman feels deprived of the love that she has been taught to expect. This is why love problems are universal in psychotherapy—the woman almost always finds her love experiences a disappointment and comes to get more out of love and life.

A number of examples have been given in this chapter of women who are hurt or frustrated or depressed because of the love disappointments in their lives. Many more could be given, but it suffices to note that women in our culture almost universally feel unhappy in their love lives.

Examples have been given to show that the woman's dissatisfaction in love can be traced back to a bad relationship with her mother. Life is a progression from one person to another. After she leaves her mother, the girl moves on to her father. If the relationship with her mother is bad, as is so often the case, she sees her father as a savior; in adult life this translates into a deep romantic attachment. Because this romantic attachment rests upon the earlier unhappiness with her mother, sooner or later it breaks up and the woman reexperiences the feelings of rejection and disappointment that she felt earlier in life. To elucidate this process and help the woman get over it makes up the essence of the psychotherapeutic encounter.

4 | Sexuality

Traditionally, in Western culture, women have been constrained to repress their sexuality on pain of condemnation or, in some cases, death. This is reflected in the frequency with which women present sexual problems to a therapist.

It is instructive to review the history of attitudes toward women's sexuality in America, as they show the diversity of problems that women have faced. These attitudes are extensively analyzed by Myrna Lewis in her "History of Female Sexuality in the United States" (1980). Lewis notes that in the colonial era, the sexual customs of American Indian women varied tremendously, but in general unmarried girls had considerable sexual freedom, while married women were expected to remain faithful to their husbands. Specific customs, however, varied in different sections of the country.

Among the New England Puritans, by contrast, marital sex was considered a necessary evil, tolerated in order to conceive children and avoid nonmarital sexual temptations. Still, many Puritans were unable to meet their own exacting sexual standards.

In the middle colonies, a much more relaxed sexual standard prevailed. Among some groups such as the Pennsylvania Dutch, premarital sex was an accepted social custom. In the southern colonies, sexuality for women was influenced by slavery and the fact that the less sexually strict Anglican Church of England rather than Puritanism was the dominant religious influence. A sexual double standard existed between white men and women, with many men openly keeping black and white slave and servant women as mistresses.

Sexuality

A new force arose toward the end of the nineteenth century with the expansion of the middle class and an accompanying concern with propriety, conformity, and social acceptability. This force was symbolized as "Mrs. Grundy," the nosy neighbor who would judge improper behavior, especially sexual behavior.

The first public discussion of female sexuality began in the United States about 1880, when books on "sexual physiology" and "sexual hygiene" began to appear. Many of these books presented the nineteenth century American woman as congenitally incapable of experiencing complete sexual satisfaction and peculiarly liable to sexual anesthesia. Dr. William Acton, one of the most widely quoted sex experts of his time, stated that "as a general rule, a modest woman seldom desires any sexual gratification for herself. She submits to her husband, but only to please him, and, but for the desire of maternity, would far rather be relieved from his attention" (Lewis, 1980, p. 22).

One factor that helped to account for this theory of female frigidity was a change in social attitudes toward women. Female labor was no longer so desperately required as before, and the social model became that of the idle housewife, whose main function was to keep a home and enhance the conspicuous consumption of her upwardly mobile husband. (This is the model that Thorstein Veblen was later to lampoon in his book *The Theory of the Leisure Class*). In addition, a movement was afoot for various reasons to limit the number of children and, of course, the number of pregnancies. Thomas Malthus had already come along, raising the specter of overpopulation destroying the world—a vision that helped give rise to the modern birth control movement. A further interesting influence on female sexuality was the belief that simultaneous orgasm on the part of both partners increased the possibility of conception, which led some women to hold back orgasm as a birth control technique.

Venereal disease also had a profound effect on the behavior of women, with estimates that as many as 30 percent of men and women eventually contracted a venereal infection. In the nineteenth century most women had only two vocational choices: marriage and prostitution. Prostitution carried high risks of venereal disease, and married women who did not acquire venereal disease directly often acquired it from their husbands, who had been with prostitutes. Other physical ailments and diseases also took a toll on women. For example, a mysterious disease known as chlorosis afflicted young girls in the nineteenth century, making them chronically ill.

Perhaps the greatest impediment to healthy sexual expression in nineteenth century women was horror of masturbation (variously called self-abuse, self-pollution, or the solitary vice). Young girls were subject to an immense number of restrictions (evidently often ignored) to help them avoid masturbatory temptations. Scoldings and physical restraint were the most common preventive techniques. Both clitoridectomy and cauterization (burning or blistering of the spine, thighs, or genitals) were accepted procedures. The clitoridectomy was introduced in England in 1858 by Isaac Baker Brown, a respected London surgeon who later became president of the Medical Society of London. Although he was eventually expelled by the English Obstetrical Society for his work and condemned by a majority of American doctors, clitoridectomy and cauterization continued to be used on thousands of females in America for many years. Even baby girls were considered dangerous to themselves; in 1905 a toddler of two and a half had her clitoris removed and a major pediatric textbook mentions such practices as late as 1935 (Lewis, 1980).

In the light of later findings that self-exploration and masturbation in early childhood are important in enabling females to learn to respond easily and pleasurably to sexual stimulation, the massive repression of masturbation in the nineteenth century explains a good part of whatever difficulties the Victorian female had.

It is important to note that American women apparently were not an easy lot to repress. The New England sexual ethic was confronted by a female population that was rambunctious and headstrong and geographically strung out along the entire eastern coastline. The sheer variety of cultures from which these women came and the need for their active participation in settling the New World made their control difficult. In the latter part of the nineteenth century and early twentieth century, when it looked as though large numbers of women were finally settling into more traditional female roles, the birth control movement, the women's

Sexuality

suffrage campaign, the free love movement, and finally the need for female labor in factories began to counterbalance the influences of John Calvin, the Mathers, and "Mrs. Grundy" (Dubois and Ruiz, 1990).

Around the early part of the twentieth century, the study of human sexuality began flourishing as part of the general movement toward human liberation. The first major changes in public thinking about female sexuality came from the efforts of Havelock Ellis and Sigmund Freud. Ellis introduced the general public to the revolutionary idea that women were as interested in sex as men and even had, in his opinion, a more complex and all-inclusive sexuality. Freud contributed the all-important observation that excessive sexual repression, the hallmark of his day, led to actual physical illness. The impact of the more liberal attitudes toward female sexuality began to be reflected in marriage manuals, which proliferated all through the twentieth century. Pleasure rather than procreation began to be advocated as a model for women, first within marriage, then in general life.

Female sex surveys began to appear. The first was the Mosher survey (Degler, 1974), which gives the first glimpse we have of nineteenth-century women talking about their sexual feelings and responses. Many were surprisingly frank in their enjoyment of sexuality, even though most held the typical nineteenth century view that sex was primarily for reproductive purposes.

A real breakthrough came in the 1950s with the work of Kinsey in his two volumes on male and female sexuality. Kinsey showed that violation of the conventional sexual mores was widespread. Premarital intercourse, masturbation, and homosexuality were much more common than was previously thought, and younger generations of women were more sexually active than their mothers and grandmothers had been. He also showed that large numbers of women failed to reach orgasm through intercourse alone. He did not quite understand his own findings, asserting that vaginal orgasm was a Freudian myth—a view that was completely discarded when the Masters and Johnson report came along in the 1960s.

Masters and Johnson found that human sexual response was similar for both sexes, with vaginal lubrication seen as the neurophysiological parallel to erection in the male as a major sign of sexual arousal. They confirmed the analytic view that females are sexual human beings in and of themselves, capable of being fully equal partners with men rather than merely reacting to male initiative. This, and psychoanalytic thought, opened the way to the realization that women could have sexual pleasure in many ways and brought a new feeling of liberation into the sexual code. Thus, a new era of sexual freedom dawned, confirming Freud's prediction in 1898 that it would take mankind 100 years to overcome its sexual repressions.

In the early 1980s, the boundaries of sexual freedom were challenged by the sudden appearance of AIDS, which has forced people to be more careful about their sexual pleasures. As of the early 1990s, a new integration of sex and love was still being sought.

Thus, the sexual conflicts seen today run the gamut from the old-style repression to the new-style promiscuity, with all shades of variations in between. While sexual problems are still common in any psychotherapeutic practice, there is no one set problem that appears, as in Freud's day.

Rejection of Sex

Hannah, a forty-five-year-old nurse, could have been one of Freud's patients. Still a virgin, she had only kissed two men in her entire life. She was a devoutly religious woman; had she been a Catholic, she would certainly have become a nun.

Hannah was the youngest of four children; the others were boys. Brought up in a family atmosphere that placed little stress on sex, she did not engage in any sex play in her adolescence. Instead, she focused on the body and its ills, becoming a nurse. After graduating as a nurse, Hannah accepted a tour of duty in the Far East, where there were virtually no eligible white men; in other words, she chose a setting where she would be "safe" from sex.

Upon returning to this country, Hannah found that her father was seriously ill. In order to take care of him, she moved to Florida, where he had retired. There she tended him night and day; her tasks included washing and cleaning his genital area. Just like Freud's patients, this sick-nursing of her father intensified her in-

Sexuality

cestuous wishes and her consequent fear of sex. She never made any effort to see why she stayed away from sex, just accepted it as part of herself.

In her work as a nurse, Hannah was assigned to help new mothers take care of their babies. This made her exceedingly nervous, and she conceived the idea of leaving her profession. She went to a vocational counselor, who advised therapy, especially since she was experiencing increasing anxiety with her clients.

The therapy reduced Hannah's anxiety to some extent but did not change her sexual pattern; that was too fixed. Even in a group where everyone else was enjoying a sex life, she reacted by making fun of them, saying, "What do you get out of all this sex?" She made a brief foray into another, less developed group, where the leader would go around kissing the women, all of whom were as inhibited as Hannah. Out of this came one date, which she handled in a peculiar way. She made the man wait downstairs instead of inviting him up to her apartment. When he took her home, she allowed him to give her one kiss and ended the evening abruptly.

Although therapy was partly successful in reducing Hannah's anxiety, her absolute refusal to have anything to do with men limited the result. Evidently, she had begun therapy too late; the attempt to change at her age ran up against the rigidity of her character structure, and she terminated therapy after about five years with a minimal amount of change.

In the case of Ingrid, who was also a nurse, the therapy had a more favorable outcome. Ingrid was thirty-five when she started and still a virgin. She was the third child in a midwestern family that was emotionally distant. For example, her parents had two television sets, and each parent would watch his or her own set.

Before analysis, Ingrid had one close relationship with a doctor colleague. They would spend their time playing cards endlessly, neither one ever exchanging any intimacies with the other. For a long time, Ingrid had been content with this empty contact.

In the course of the analysis, Ingrid became dissatisfied with the emptiness of her life, especially when she heard the stories of others in her group. She broke up with her doctor friend because of his lack of libido and began to go out with other men. Eventually she was able to start a sex life with one of the men whom she dated. Her work improved and she felt better all around. In her specialty she was even able to write a book, which provided much gratification.

One love affair brought her very close to marriage, but at the last minute the man backed out. Nevertheless, Ingrid felt that she had made a significant advance toward maturity.

Here again, where the analysis was begun relatively late in life, the rigidity of the client's character structure played a significant role. Sex is not manna from heaven, but the capacity to engage in a sexual relationship at a fairly early age (in one's twenties, for example) is an indication that the woman has the capacity to change, even if circumstances do not provide the change sought for.

The Adjustment Neurosis

Ingrid's case illustrates the psychoanalytic proposition that the degree of mental health of any individual cannot be inferred from his or her external adjustment but has to be gauged by the inner equilibrium.

This leads us to the most fundamental psychoanalytic contribution of all, the unconscious. As early as 1900, in *The Interpretation of Dreams,* Freud wrote, "The unconscious is the true psychical reality; in its innermost nature it is as much unknown to us as the reality of the external world, and it is as incompletely presented by the data of consciousness as is the external world by the combination of the sense organs" (Freud, [1899] 1953, p. 603).

This position on reality and the unconscious, which underlies all psychoanalytic theorizing, leads to the distinction between the adjustment neurosis and the maladjustment neurosis. Traditional psychiatry understood only the maladjustment neurosis; it had no inkling of the adjustment neurosis.

Following out this line of thought allows us to understand a case like Ingrid. She was adjusted to her world, even successful in it. But inwardly, because of her rejection of sexual experience, she was seriously disturbed, in a certain sense even psychotic. It is the delineation of this adjustment neurosis that has attracted people to psychoanalysis and made it such a potent tool in understanding the world in which we live.

These principles help to explain the difficulties of Jane, a

Sexuality

college professor married to another college professor. Jane and her husband had an extensive social life with a great many friends and acquaintances. Outwardly they seemed perfectly happy; only one thing was missing: a family.

Actually, the courtship of Jane and her husband had been quite stormy; several times there had been threats of a breakup. Jane, dissatisfied with herself, decided to undergo analysis. She went to a man who was a refugee from Nazi Germany. Because of Nazism, he had consciously decided against having children. When he finally emigrated to the United States, in his late forties, he and his wife decided it was too late to change their minds about having children. He pressed upon Jane the view that it was not necessary to have children to be happy; he had also drifted into a kind of analysis in which sex was of no importance (he was tweaking Freud's nose). Jane and her husband had sex less and less frequently until they indulged in it perhaps once every four or five months. Jane finished her analysis without having penetrated very deeply into her life.

It was no accident that Jane's husband started his own analysis with this statement to his analyst: "I want to make two things plain. I will never become dependent on you, and I will never have any children." His own father had deserted him when he was a baby, and he had become terribly dependent on his mother, which created a long, conflicted relationship.

The life of no sex and no children gradually became more and more intolerable to both parties. Jane became steadily more depressed, and her husband at one point acquired a mistress, a vivacious young woman who worked in his office. Although he did not really wish it, his mistress pressed him to divorce Jane. Jane was amazed when he finally requested a divorce, although she might have anticipated it given how nongratifying their life was. At this point, Jane became markedly depressed and sought help from a man who was an expert on depression.

Sexual Frustration in Marriage

As women get older, they find it increasingly difficult to derive satisfaction from sex. Unmarried women are frightened off by the traditional taboos of the culture, while married women have sex less and less often. According to Kinsey (1953), some 25 percent of his sample in the fifty-one to fifty-five age group never had sex at all (p. 351). For women who were married in their late teens, the average weekly incidence of marital coitus began at nearly 3 (pp. 348-349). This dropped to 2.2 per week by age thirty, to 1.5 per week by age forty, to 1.0 per week by age fifty, and to 0.60 per week (once in twelve days) by age sixty.

Women's desires for sexual satisfaction, however, do not diminish at the rate indicated by these figures, with the consequence that many women are condemned to a life of perpetual sexual frustration. No doubt this is changing in light of the greater sexual freedom accorded to women nowadays, but exact statistics are missing, and it can safely be assumed that women, married or not, will still have sex less often as they get older, though there are many exceptions (Blumstein and Schwartz, 1983). In view of the inadequacy of marriage in providing women with sexual satisfaction, it is not surprising that extramarital affairs are indulged in more often as time goes on.

Karen, a forty-five-year-old mother of two, came to analysis because of stomach trouble and marital frustration. She was the youngest of four children of wealthy parents who had died young, leaving her to be brought up by relatives. Karen experimented with various professional possibilities—social work, medicine, art—but could never find herself in any of them.

Sexually she remained a virgin until marriage. One reason for this was that her voice sounded very masculine, so that men were not attracted to her. Finally, at the age of thirty-six, she met a man who seemed sufficiently attractive for marriage. He was much older than she—close to fifty—but he was a struggling artist, and she wished to help him develop his talent. Neither was really in love with the other; the marriage was one of convenience more than anything else. Two children came.

Karen had never really enjoyed sex, but she submitted to it. When she was about forty-five, her husband lost all sexual interest in her and began to seek out other women. The two lived in a bohemian section of New York where extramarital sex was common, so that his behavior was not so surprising. In addition, he

Sexuality

claimed that as an artist he needed the stimulus of frequent sex to pursue his art properly, and she was just not suitable.

Masochistically, Karen accepted this judgment and devoted herself to her children. Sexually frustrated, she also began to drink, at times rather heavily. She was eager to have an extramarital affair, but no man approached her.

Then Karen developed stomach trouble, diagnosed as a pre-ulcerous condition. In the medical tradition of that day, she was treated with various medications that did not help much. In her despair, she turned to analysis.

The first analyst she went to tried the bizarre technique of pounding her stomach with his hands. This produced some pleasurable reactions that teased her more than they gratified her. She also decided to go to an analytic institute and became a psychoanalyst.

Partially in reaction to the physical manipulation, she began to seek out sexual experience more actively. However, by then she was about fifty, and she could not succeed in finding a lover.

In the meantime, her husband had become impotent. He would pinch the bottom of any woman he liked at a party and say to her, "If I were only potent, I would have an affair with you." Sometimes he actually succeeded in having an affair, never bothering to conceal it from his wife, which in turn frustrated her even more.

In a second analysis, Karen was able to get over her stomach problem, curb her drinking, and progress toward her goal of becoming an analyst. Unfortunately, just when she seemed to be succeeding at her various goals, she developed cancer and died within a few weeks.

Sexual Experimentation

I have described a number of women who were deprived of sexual pleasure by the circumstances of their lives and became seriously depressed by the deprivation. On the other side are those women who will not put up with the deprivation but will do anything to break out of it. Here are some examples.

Lucy

Lucy came to therapy because of constant anxieties about her body. She was a music teacher who had to stand on a platform in order to conduct, and she felt frightened that members of the audience could see her underwear from below. In addition, she had unusual tastes in underwear and feared that these would be discovered.

The background of these fears was a family with a rather violent father and an extremely passive mother. Lucy was one of six children, five girls and a boy. The father was a businessman who indulged himself at home by getting drunk, scaring all his daughters, and acting seductively toward some. One daughter became a prostitute, one a kept woman, one committed suicide. Only one sister had a seemingly normal life.

As long as she could remember, Lucy had suffered from fears of being seduced. When she was five years old, one of her teachers told her to play with his penis; when this was discovered, he was immediately dismissed. Then, when she was nine, a brother-in-law, much older than she, seduced her into taking off her underpants and allowing him to take a picture of her vagina. He kept this picture for a long time, and even as an adult she was terrified that he would send this picture to the education authorities (she was a teacher by then), who would dismiss her for lewd activities. (The natural question of how the board of education could distinguish her vagina from that of other little girls did not occur to her; primary was the terrible fear of having her secret sexual desires discovered.)

Once she reached adolescence, Lucy began to experiment more actively with sex. At first it was homosexual play with a girlfriend; then she moved on to men. She and her girlfriend would pick up men and have sex with them on the spot—in a hallway, on the street, but never at home. Then Lucy would sit in class all week, frightened that she might be pregnant since she did not know enough about contraception to use anything if the man did not have a condom. Several times she contracted a venereal disease; three times she got pregnant and had abortions. All this time she suffered terrible fears, which at bottom went back to the wish to have sex with her father. It was even rumored that her father *had* had sex with one of his daughters (the one who later became a prostitute).

Lucy's family knew nothing of her sexual escapades, which continued for years. At one point, she met a man with whom she fell in love. Unfortunately, the feelings were not reciprocated, and he even turned her into a prostitute, getting his friends to pay him for sex with her. This proved to be too much for Lucy; and she broke off with him.

When Lucy was twenty, she met the man whom she was later to marry. He was thrilled by her sexual openness, so he took to her immediately. During a lovers' quarrel, when they broke up for a while, he took up with a dance hall hostess. Eventually they got back together again and married. There was one child, a boy. When he was about seven, he developed a urinary problem (excessive urination). She took him to various doctors, one of whom mistakenly thought that the boy's penis was too small and advised her to watch him constantly to make sure that his penis developed to a normal size.

That was all the encouragement Lucy needed. She became very attached to the boy and was constantly preoccupied with the size of his penis. She also became very seductive with him, asking him, for example, to put her brassiere on for her; often she would come out of the bathroom naked, knowing that he was there to see her. Later the boy became so incensed at this almost overt seduction that he once tore her dress from top to bottom, which she properly took as a sign to stop trying to make him her lover.

Lucy's marriage was a stormy one. She was always eager to redecorate the house, to which her husband objected. Over and over they would discuss divorce, sometimes even going to a lawyer to draw up papers, but then they would cancel it at the last minute. Eventually things calmed down, and they stayed together all their lives.

Sexually, Lucy remained frustrated and dissatisfied all her life. She could never reach a vaginal orgasm, although she tried. She preferred anal intercourse, even though her husband abhorred it.

Eventually Lucy gave up some of her excessive need for control and reached a fairly happy medium in her marriage. The boy grew up with serious problems, which he resolved with therapy when he was an adult.

Marilyn

Swinging, or parties where everyone is free to have sex with everyone else, for a while became almost a national pastime. Gilbert

Bartell, a sociologist, has published an interesting report on swingers, whom he studied close-up (Bartell, 1971). His main finding is the noncommital one that swingers are just like other people; all they want is more sex. This seems improbable, and psychoanalytic research has to be called on to clarify why some people go in for swinging while others do not.

Marilyn, the daughter of a physician, had a breakdown in her adolescence and was hospitalized and given shock treatment. She recovered from this breakdown without gaining much insight. She then married and entered into a life of great promiscuity. Primarily she was eager to show how liberated she was, in contrast to her strait-laced parents.

Marilyn found a swingers' organization and began to go to arranged swings with her husband, a research scientist. She did not experience any pleasure in the swings, but she was proud of her willingness to try anything. This swinging life went on for quite a while, until she tired of it and gave it up. Before she could give it up, however, she had to experience a homosexual encounter. For a while, her greatest thrill was to lie between a man and a woman, preferably married, and alternatively have sex with each of them. This was clearly a return to her childhood, when she was forbidden to get into the parental bed.

Interestingly, Marilyn was quite frightened by her husband's wish to go to therapy. In swings she could watch her husband have sex with another woman, but when he wanted to entrust his thoughts to another person, she became very jittery.

Norma

Norma was a typical example of today's adolescent girl. Her mother early in life went into a deep depression, from which she never recovered. Her father was away from home much of the time, apparently carrying on with other women.

Unsupervised, Norma drifted into the wrong crowd. Actually, she felt terrible because she was left alone too much and sought to take revenge on her parents by her unruly behavior. It was not long before she was openly taking drugs, drinking, and having sex. For Norma, sex was the expression of a kind of animal-like longing

Sexuality

for touching and affection of any kind. At one point she latched onto a young man with a criminal record, but she managed to give that up fairly quickly.

Naturally, school meant little to Norma. She did well when she applied herself, but most of the time she could not apply herself. Everybody who knew her saw her as a lost soul. When last seen, at twenty-five, she was working as a cocktail waitress, and the future did not look bright for her.

Olivia

Olivia was the youngest of four children and the only girl. All her brothers suffered deep afflictions. One was murdered in a homosexual affair; another made a deeply unhappy marriage to a woman who was pregnant by another man. The third was an inveterate gambler.

Olivia's father had spent years as an alcoholic, and her mother seemed to be both retarded and chronically depressed. Before Olivia was born, there was another girl who had died at the age of two and a half years. "Her blood ran cold" was her mother's explanation for the death. Olivia's mother was so fearful that something would happen to Olivia that she would wake her up at night to say to her, "What is my maiden name?" Olivia's mother died from a fall while she was sitting on her porch; the chair toppled over and she was killed.

It is not surprising that with such a family background Olivia would emerge with many psychological problems. Before analysis, she had never had a room of her own; as a child, her parents hung a curtain across an interior opening and called the alcove her room. As an adult, she always shared an apartment with other women.

When Olivia came to analysis, she was obsessed with the idea of being raped. Every man she saw was a potential rapist. Actually, she was rather promiscuous; many times she would go to the park, pick out a man, and take him home to have sex with her.

Olivia's rape fear involved an interesting story. When she was twenty, she and a girlfriend hitchhiked their way around the country. Many times they would be picked up by truck drivers, who often wanted to have sex with them. This the girls refused, although they would allow the men to play with their breasts.

One time in Mississippi, they were picked up by two men who took them to a rather secluded spot in the hills, where the couples separated. The man Olivia went off with pulled a knife on her and forced her to have sex. Apparently, her girlfriend, who went off with the other man, was not approached in this way.

When Olivia got back to town, she filed charges of rape against the man who had picked her up. A jury trial was held, and the man was found guilty and fined $1. Olivia felt totally humiliated by this. In her later fantasies about rape there was embodied the idea of revenge against this man, or some other man like him. Sometimes when she took a man home and he wanted to have sex, she would say, "What do you think I am? A whore?" Then she would kick him out. At other times, she would go to bed with the man.

Two things were in Olivia's favor: she was a good artist and worked at it, and she persisted in trying to change herself. Eventually she made a surprisingly good adjustment, with a happy marriage to a lawyer that greatly stabilized her everyday life. She went on to get a Ph.D. degree in her field. In her case, the extreme promiscuity that characterized her in the beginning of therapy was a cry for contact, a wish to feel the warm embrace of some other person.

Pat

The same dynamic wish for contact came out in the analysis of Pat, a thirty-year-old actress. Pat was the younger of two sisters; the older sister had always been the dominant one. Although her mother had married late, the children came when she was still in her thirties. Evidently, she had not wanted Pat very much because her early life was filled with stories of terrible cruelty. For example, when she was a little girl, her mother would punish her by locking her in a closet all night.

As Pat grew up, her adjustment consisted of clinging to her older sister. In college, when she was first separated from her sister,

Sexuality

she became completely promiscuous, accepting almost any boy that came along. This continued into the therapy.

After some years of therapy Pat got married. This seemingly terminated the therapy satisfactorily, but ten years later, still married and with three children, she came back in a highly emotional state. She heard voices directing her to do this and that, and she had the fixed idea that her husband, whose factory was well out of town, was running a brothel. As proof of this, she said she had read in the papers that businessmen all employed prostitutes to advance their business, and it could be assumed that her husband was doing the same.

Because of this delusion about him, she wanted to leave the marriage and go back to her mother, a move that the therapist managed to restrain. In her despair, one day she took a knife and plunged it into her chest, explaining afterwards that she wanted to cut her husband out of her heart. The surgeon said that if the knife had been half an inch away from where it was, she would have died.

Subsequent hospitalization led to some improvement, but still all Pat wanted was to go home to her mother. One day her husband gave in and took her home, a move that ended the therapy. Back home, Pat regressed further, and when last heard from she was hospitalized with little hope of recovery.

In this case, as in the previous one, the promiscuity of the patient's early years was essentially a wish for contact with the mother. Since the wish for contact is paramount in such cases, the particular arrangements made about sex make little difference, and arguments about the best social rules for sex likewise matter little. It is important to know that while promiscuity does not always cover up a deep disturbance, in many cases it does.

The Older Woman

As a result of this century's improvements in public health, many women at fifty have the physical resilience that women formerly had at forty, and women at sixty seem as young as their mothers were at fifty. Women now work well into their fifties and sixties, sometimes even into their seventies and eighties. Moreover, improvements in medical knowledge and practice have banished some diseases and made others much less common.

With these improvements in health come many other advantages. Older women no longer need to be so completely protective of themselves as they once were. Today, even women in their fifties and sixties will demand a divorce from an unresponsive or brutal man rather than face a life that goes on in unceasing troubles. Many of these women who see divorce as better than a bad marriage will tell you that they expect to remarry, and many of them do. (See Chapter Ten for an extended discussion of the divorced woman.)

What is true physically is also true psychologically. An acquaintance of mine once threw a wake for herself when she hit forty; thereafter, she went steadily downhill. Such an attitude is seen much more rarely today now that women have acquired more freedom to experiment with different styles of life. For example, whereas sexuality was once virtually forbidden to "decent" women, many women now enjoy a new lease on life in their late forties, including an active sexual life. Even the pattern of older women dating younger men is by no means so rare as it used to be.

Several cases have already been cited in this chapter showing women who made great readjustments in their attitudes toward sexuality and the younger generation as they got older and who refused to tolerate the bad treatment they had been receiving for years from their spouses or lovers. A case in point is Karen, who decided to become an analyst after going into analysis herself and who was open to the idea of seeking a lover after her marriage turned sour. Unfortunately, she died before she could reach her goals.

Myrna's life moved along different lines. At twenty-three she married an older man, a powerful lawyer, with whom she had two children but whom she did not love. It was then that she met a younger man, with whom she fell deeply in love. He reciprocated, but her husband refused to give her a divorce. A generation earlier, she might have given up on life, but she did not want to. She left her husband and two daughters and moved in with her lover.

Her husband, who carried a lot of weight in the court system, had her followed and discovered her in flagrante delicto. Myrna felt checked but not checkmated and continued her life with her lover,

Sexuality

with whom she had a life that was both sociable and sexually active. Her husband, who was a brutal, authoritarian man, responded by suing her for custody of the children. Because of his wealth and influence, he won the custody battle.

By this time the children were young adolescents. After her husband gained custody of them, Myrna fought back. She made sure that she obeyed every command of the court and left it to her daughters to rebel. A series of encounters developed that hit the headlines in her town newspapers, making her a temporary heroine. Photographs were taken showing how her daughters rebelled each time she brought them to her ex-husband, as she was required to do. The girls simply refused to stay with their father, whom they did not like because of his authoritarian manner.

The sexual may very well be, as Freud insisted in his early days, the precursor of the psychic. It is striking that both Karen and Myrna were able to achieve a degree of sexual maturation that was previously unknown for most woman.

5 | Motherhood

Essential to a woman's well-being is her biological capacity to be a mother. From her earliest years, she is programmed both psychologically and physiologically to become a mother. As a toddler, she is encouraged to play with dolls and pretend to be a mother. At around eight or nine, the breast buds appear, indicating that breasts are ready to grow. At around age thirteen, the girl begins to menstruate and is physically capable of bearing children, though women today rarely do that at so early an age. (It is not so long ago that thirteen-year-old girls did marry and have families; both my own grandmothers married at thirteen, and each had thirteen children.) In her early teens, the girl develops various secondary sexual characteristics, and by fifteen or sixteen she is fully developed. Menstruation continues until age fifty or so; its stoppage signifies the end of the childbearing capacity. (Analytically, we call menstruation a frustrated pregnancy.)

In other words, biologically the girl's whole life from birth on is centered around pregnancy and becoming a mother. The woman who does not have children is often looked upon with sorrow and compassion. While there are many other needs and desires that play a role in a woman's life, the ability to become a mother remains biological bedrock, no matter how refined and sophisticated we become. It is essential for the race to survive, and survival is one of the strongest of all forces in evolution.

Problems arise for the woman at every stage of the mothering cycle, from menstruation through pregnancy, birth, and the development of the mother-child relationship. At present there is a reac-

Motherhood

tionary tendency to strike down the *Roe* v. *Wade* decision of the Supreme Court and make abortion illegal again. Should that happen and be enforced, it would make for enormous, possibly catastrophic changes in women's lives; many of us still remember the dangerous illegal abortions that were performed before the Supreme Court ruling, abortions that maimed and killed many helpless women. The psychoanalyst Devereux, in his study of abortion in primitive societies, has shown how the fear of childbirth and pregnancy runs through all cultures. The practice of abortion is prominent in all societies, which makes abortion a universal problem. For a child to be born, the welfare of both mother and child must be carefully safeguarded, which means that the whole structure of society still comes to center around the mother-child dyad (Devereux, 1955).

Women are troubled by every step of the growth process leading to motherhood. Many little girls want to be tomboys, that is, boys. Many others play at being a little mother, for example, by hiding pillows under their dresses to make believe that they are pregnant. Psychoanalysis has shown that the wish to have a child by her father develops very early in the little girl and plays a decisive role in her psychological makeup. While many modern women have attacked the analytic concepts of penis envy and castration anxiety, these terms are descriptive, not prescriptive. The Freudian schema for female psychosexual development, while it has been modified in many ways, is still one of the best guidelines for the development profile of the woman.

It is not surprising that there is a vast literature dealing with the many phases of the mother-child relationship. In particular, Freudians became convinced about 1940 that TLC (tender loving care) is as essential to the development of a healthy child as bread and milk. At every stage of the developmental line of motherhood, there have been suggestions for a mechanical arrangement of the situation. For example, there is Leboyer's suggestion that right after birth the baby should lie naked on the stomach of the mother, and that even an hour of such tenderness will ensure healthy growth forever. Like all other mechanical arrangements, this suggestion has been rejected by most analysts; studies have been done that actually disprove it. What psychoanalytic theory emphasizes above all is that there is no mechanical road to nirvana; the prime requirement of the mother is to be loving and understanding.

Mothers have been categorized in various ways, depending mainly on their attitudes toward their children. Apart from her capacity to love, perhaps a mother's most important capacity is her ability to recognize her child's needs. In "Three Essays on the Theory of Sexuality," Freud made the point that the mother fulfills her psychological task by teaching the child to love ([1905] 1953). The chief danger is that paternal love will become too strong, thus doing the child harm. In ordinary language, the child is *spoiled* by making the child incapable in later life of temporarily doing without love or of being content with a smaller amount of it (p. 223).

It is on these simple ideas that the whole theory of psychoanalysis rests. Children learn to love from the treatment accorded them by their parents, especially the mother. If they do not learn love, they become disturbed. Rohner (1975) has shown that these observations apply universally. He notes that the warm mother "produces a more lovable infant, that is easier to be with because it cries less, is less fretful and is less fussy. Also, she can continue over time to be relaxed and pleasant with her child, but the non-nurturant mother is preparing her own less satisfactory future" (p. 120).

In recent years, there has been a kind of rebellion against motherhood, the sad consequences of which are pictured in dire terms. In *A Lesser Life* (1986), Sylvia Hewlett has shown that these women are in rebellion against something within themselves: to become a mother is the one problem they cannot face. In spite of the attacks on motherhood, however, in 1980 only 10 percent of all women aged forty to forty-four were childless. More women are having at least one child than ever before.

Happy and Unhappy Mothers

Although there are many ways of classifying mothers (Brody, 1956), one obvious pair of classifications is not usually found: those women who are happy as mothers, and those who are not. Throughout hu-

Motherhood

man history, the most common adjustment women had to make was to motherhood; some found it pleasant, some did not.

To pursue the idea of grouping mothers in accordance with how much pleasure they derive from mothering, as well as what effect they have on their children, we shall present two cases, one of a "good" mother, the other of a "bad" one, and then go on from there. Naturally, the woman's relationship to her husband plays a significant role in these cases and must be considered in the total adjustment of the woman.

Rachel

Rachel came from a large family, with two brothers and three sisters; she was in the middle. Her father was a successful businessman. Rachel's schooling was limited to high school plus a few years of community college. At eighteen, she met her future husband, Sam, who later became a successful insurance agent. The two were married when Rachel was twenty-one.

The marriage was a happy one and produced four children, one of whom had juvenile diabetes. The other three grew up well and had successful careers. All married in their early twenties. One was gifted as a writer and published a number of books, one of which won a literary prize. The others had families and lived fairly happy lives. Just as she had been happy as a mother, Rachel was happy as a grandmother; when she died at eighty, she had fourteen grandchildren who loved her dearly.

No doubt many will be surprised that such happy lives and happy families still exist, but they do. Ideally, the possibility for such happy outcomes in the individual and the family is interfered with only by disturbed social or political conditions, neither of which entered into Rachel's case.

Shirley

Shirley was in most respects the exact opposite of Rachel. She was the third of ten children. Her mother was a clerical worker who was deserted by her husband when the children were still small. Shirley grew up in the midst of terrible poverty and unhappiness. Her mother became very bitter about her lot in life and took it out on the children.

Rejected at home, Shirley fell in love at fifteen and became pregnant right away. Abortion was still illegal at that time, so she had a back-alley abortion that was quite painful and from which it took her years to recover.

Finally she did marry, at twenty-one, and had two children, a boy and a girl. Both were healthy but with many emotional conflicts. There were constant fights between Shirley and her children; the boy eventually took to drugs, and the girl began to experiment sexually at an early age. The battles with the children grew steadily more intense. Eventually, both children left Shirley, and she had to adjust herself to a dreary, lonely old age.

Melanie

Shirley's sister Melanie could also be mentioned here. Frightened as a girl, she still managed to marry young. She had one child, a boy, but his life was a disaster. Always a shy, withdrawn boy, he became steadily more withdrawn as time went on. In college he felt picked on by his physics teacher and dropped out. After college he tried various things, and each one he could handle well up to a certain point; then he would suddenly quit. This loss of interest became so strong that he eventually withdrew from everything until it was clear that he was virtually a textbook schizophrenic. The boy's battle with his parents reached violent proportions, and at one time or another he attacked both of them. One day he collapsed on the street, where he was found by a policeman and taken to the nearest psychiatric hospital. As is so often the case, the psychiatrists there had little understanding of schizophrenia and treated him with shock therapy and inappropriate drugs. He was sent to a custodial hospital, where he eventually died.

These three examples illustrate various problems of motherhood. Without speculating about genetics, it can still be said that a warm, sensitive mother tends to produce a responsive, outgoing child, while a cold, insensitive mother will produce a child with varying degrees of pathology.

The textbook classifications of mothers as schizophrenic,

Motherhood

phallic, possessive, and the like give us some idea of what disturbed women are like, but it is really necessary to study a woman's whole life history to get a full picture of the mother-child situation. Here are some further examples of disturbed mother-child relationships.

Tamara

Tamara withdrew from her husband after their baby boy was born. Although her husband was a patient, tolerant man, she could not stand being married and finally left him, only to come back to him a year later.

Tamara's background was very traumatic. Her father was a physician who pulled back from social life and became a complete alcoholic before he was forty. He was only able to maintain himself as a physician because he had an appointment in the coroner's office that required very little attention on his part.

There were four children in Tamara's family, the others being boys. When the Vietnam War broke out, her younger brother, who was the family's favorite, volunteered for active duty. In Vietnam his plane was sabotaged and he was killed. The resultant grief engulfed the entire family. Tamara's mother, in particular, became psychotic, lost herself in musings about the afterlife and the spirit world, and was no longer available as a mother. Her father just buried himself in drink.

Tamara was courted by several men in her home town, but nothing ever clicked. She went away to a larger city to study painting, at which she had shown some talent. There she met a young man who was devoted but unglamorous, and she married him. She was never very happy in this marriage but she tolerated it because she felt that she could not do any better in life.

When her son was born, she became frantically devoted to him, and for ten years nothing else mattered to her. Sexual feelings for the boy developed, which made her go to a therapist, where it was discovered that she had also had strong sexual feelings for the brother who was killed in the war. Despite therapy, these sexual feelings grew stronger. Finally she could tolerate it no longer and ran away with the boy to another city. In effect, she had married her son.

Obviously, this could not continue, and after a while she came back to her husband, who had waited patiently for her. As the boy grew up, her feelings came under better control, and she was realistic enough to know that she had to give up her strong attachment to him. This she was able to do, and she settled down to a comfortable old age with her husband. The passion was gone, but the two were congenial and got along well.

Uta

Uta had a younger brother who became schizophrenic and was hospitalized for many years, which aroused feelings of intense shame in her. Uta married, but her marriage was a very poor one; even though both she and her husband had good civil service jobs, they were constantly in debt and fought bitterly about money.

Uta's contempt for her husband carried over to her own son (she had two children, a boy and a girl). The girl she could love, but the boy became the target of near-psychotic temper tantrums. She would beat him mercilessly, always with the thought of her own brother in the back of her mind. Naturally, he grew up afraid of women and eventually became a homosexual.

Teresa

In the case of Teresa, the mother-daughter problem persisted through three generations. Teresa fought bitter battles with her daughter Nancy all through Nancy's adolescence. They were typical mother-daughter battles over Nancy staying out too late, not doing her schoolwork, and the like. What was different about them was the violence displayed by both mother and daughter.

When Nancy married, she settled into a peaceful arrangement with Teresa; but began to experience deep conflicts with her own daughter, Wilma. Wilma, like her mother, was a wild one in her adolescence, sexually promiscuous, disobedient, and defiant. She married an unsuitable man, against her parents' wishes. The battle with her parents continued for a long time, until it finally settled down when her children reached school age. Then Wilma began to have trouble with her children, especially with her older

Motherhood

daughter. The succession of troubled generations only came to a stop when Wilma's older daughter suddenly died of cancer at the age of twenty-three.

Developmentally Based Conflicts

Anna Freud has coined the useful term "developmental lines," which has become the mainstay of modern psychodynamic thinking. Every capacity goes through a developmental process until the person finally reaches maturity. The main developmental stages and their key characteristics, first described by Freud and elaborated on by many other authors, are: infancy (breast or bottle feeding, sleep and its disturbances); the toddler stage (discipline, interpersonal relations with the outside world); the Oedipal stage (sexual attraction to the opposite sex); school age (learning, growth of social life); early adolescence (conflicts with parents, sexual growth and adjustment; marriage and parenthood (moving away from the parents and into a different adult life); and grandparenthood. At each of these stages the mother can react in many different ways.

The difficulties and pleasures encountered in the management of a newborn baby, for example, have given rise to an extended literature. In one of his early papers, Freud ([1933] 1953) gives an interesting case of a young woman who was initially unable to breast-feed her children. However, after two of the births she responded to hypnotic suggestion and became able to breast-feed her infants. Although hypnosis was later abandoned by Freud, the details of the case are instructive even now. Freud himself remarked that one of the outstanding features of the case was the fact that the woman's experiences with an earlier and a later child provided controls of the therapeutic success such as is seldom obtainable.

As the time approached for the birth of the first child of her marriage (which was a happy one), the patient resolved to feed the infant herself. Although her body build seemed favorable, she did not succeed in feeding the infant satisfactorily. There was a poor flow of milk, pains were brought on when the baby was put to the breast, and the mother lost her appetite and showed an alarming unwillingness to take nourishment. In addition, her nights were agitated and sleepless. After a fortnight, in order to avoid any further risk to the mother and infant, the attempt was abandoned and the child transferred to a wet nurse. Thereupon all the mother's troubles immediately cleared up.

Three years later, a second baby was born. On this occasion, external circumstances added to the desirability of avoiding a wet nurse, but the mother's attempts at feeding the child herself seemed even less successful and provoked even more distressing symptoms than the first time. She vomited all her food, became agitated when the baby was brought to her bedside, and was completely unable to sleep. Hypnosis was tried on the fourth day. Using hypnosis, Freud said to her: "Have no fear. You will make an excellent wet nurse and the baby will thrive. Your stomach is perfectly quiet, your appetite is excellent, you are looking forward to your next meal," and so on (p. 119). After the hypnosis, she had a meal without any ill effects. However, the next day she could not hold her food down. That evening Freud told her that five minutes after his departure she would break out against her family with some acrimony, which is precisely what happened.

When Freud returned the third evening, the patient refused to have any further treatment. There was nothing more wrong with her, she said. She had an excellent appetite and plenty of milk for the baby; there was not the slightest difficulty when it was put to her breast. Her husband thought it rather queer that after Freud's departure the evening before she had clamored violently for food and had remonstrated with her mother in a way quite unlike herself. Since then, he added, everything had gone all right. The mother breast-fed her child for eight months, and Freud had many opportunities of satisfying himself that they were both doing well. However, Freud admitted that he "found it hard to understand . . . as well as annoying that no reference was ever made" to his "remarkable achievement" (p. 120).

A year later, a third child made the same demands on the mother, and she was unable to meet them as on the two previous occasions. Freud found the patient in the same condition as the year before and positively exasperated with herself because her will could do nothing against her disinclination for food and her other symptoms. The first evening's hypnosis only had the result of making her

Motherhood

feel more hopeless. Once again, after the second hypnosis the symptoms were so completely cut short that a third was not required. The child was fed without any trouble, and the mother enjoyed uninterrupted good health thenceforward.

Later the woman admitted the motive that had governed her behavior toward Freud: "I felt ashamed that a thing like hypnosis should be successful, where I myself, with all my will power, was helpless" (p. 12).

This case was one of the first that Freud ever treated on a dynamic basis. Freud obviously was in the early stages of evolving a dynamic approach to treatment. Today, by contrast, we could much more easily elicit the mother's hostility toward the baby, her fear of admitting this hostility, and whatever other fears she might have about having a baby, breast-feeding it, and the like. Nevertheless, even the early dynamic interpretations that evolved under hypnosis were of considerable help.

We could go through all the developmental lines to show that if the mother accepts the child's normal growth patterns, both she and the child feel gratified, but that if she interferes with them or objects to them too strenuously, conflict results. Some instances will be given here from different developmental stages, with later follow-up where available.

Pat

We met Pat in the last chapter as the younger of two daughters of a woman who had her children in her mid thirties. Pat learned to attach herself to her older sister, which led to her being called "Me Too." She was also quite naughty, or at least her mother thought so, and she was frequently punished. However, the punishment was severe and unusual—she would be locked in a closet all night. She remembered that this happened often from the time she was three until she was six. The sessions in the closet terrified her, but she managed to get through them.

After college, Pat became an actress and succeeded to some extent in her acting career. However, she could not endure the routine that acting aspirants have to go through in New York, making the rounds of producers, casting agencies, and the like to get a job.

In defense, she would stay home, daydreaming that someone would call her. At this period in her life, she was supported by her parents.

As luck would have it, she was a carbon copy of a famous actress, and through this similarity she was able to get a good part as an understudy to the actress. After this part, she reverted to lying around, daydreaming that something would turn up. Nothing did, so she decided to marry, discontinuing her therapy. Ten years later, she returned to therapy in a state of panic, obsessed with a variety of rather paranoid ideas. It was clear that she had broken out in a full-blown psychosis, the main content of which was sexual.

For a while, Pat's therapy went well and she seemed to be improving, but then she developed an intense hatred for her husband and wanted to go back to her mother. Restrained from doing that, she suddenly stabbed herself in the chest and came very close to killing herself. Upon her return home, she entered intensive psychotherapy, seven days a week, but nothing seemed to help her. Eventually, she wound up in a mental hospital for the rest of her life.

In this case, it was clear that the early, cruel mothering laid the basis for the later psychosis. Pat's mother was obviously acting out of rage, the roots of which, unfortunately, were never uncovered. However, this level of rage in the mother is widely seen as the most important etiological factor in the development of a paranoid schizophrenic personality such as Pat.

Beatrice

In the Oedipal period, when the child is beset by desires for both parents, but particularly for the parent of the opposite sex, innumerable conflicts beset the mother. Usually she has to either pacify the child or take a neutral stance, staying out of the storm.

Beatrice had sharp memories of being required to go upstairs when she was about five. Before then she could sit around naked or in her underwear. Then came a sharp break. All that she remembered was that she could no longer enjoy her father but had to leave him and go to bed. In this situation, the mother played a neutral role, keeping her feelings for her husband and for the child all to herself.

Motherhood

Bobbie

Sometimes the reactions of the mother during the Oedipal period take a violent form. Bobbie, an eight-year-old girl, was brought to therapy when her mother found her masturbating in front of the television set. When asked how she knew that the child was masturbating, Bobbie's mother replied that she got down on the floor and looked, noting the bright red of her child's vagina.

However, Bobbie's mother could not talk about herself. When asked questions about the family situation, she would start to cry and leave the room. Her feelings about her daughter's masturbation were obviously part of her jealousy of the child. She could not masturbate, for reasons in her past, and she took this out on her child, even hitting her especially hard.

Larry

In the latency period, the child begins to liberate himself or herself from the mother. Larry was brought to the clinic because he had begun to have bowel movements in his pants. An examination of his family brings out the conflicts inherent in it. His mother had been very dubious about marrying his father. His father had had a nervous breakdown, and Larry's mother wanted to know if that was a hereditary condition. She consulted a doctor, who did not really know but opined that the illness would carry over to the child.

When Larry was born to the couple, his mother watched him like a hawk for any signs of nervousness. Sure enough, he began to show anxiety, and she felt triumphant, blaming it on the father and feeling justified in her initial caution.

Eventually, Larry's mother began to have sex play with her son. She would lie in bed with him, asking him to caress her, and she would caress him back. This incestuous relationship preceded the period when Larry began soiling his pants. Larry's mother did not seem to be very eager to help Larry get over his symptom, probably because she did not want anyone to know about her sex play with the boy. When, as a result of the therapy, he began to show intense anxiety, she felt it best to pull him out of therapy and send him to a different school, thus abruptly ending the treatment.

When puberty comes around, the mother, instead of enjoying her child's growth, often is stimulated into all kinds of sexual fantasies. At that age, a boy may resemble his father or be fully mature and attractive in his own right. A girl may resemble her mother, which leads to feelings of rivalry and jealousy. Usually with a boy, the fantasies are sexual; with a girl, there is open rivalry. Thus, in the Jewish tradition, when the girl begins to menstruate, the mother is supposed to slap her face to make her aware that she is now capable of becoming pregnant. One of my patients recalled that when she reached this age, her grandmother smacked her so hard she hurt for days. Another recalled that when she had her first menses, she told her father, who warned her never to tell anybody about such things; this shame about her body marred her later motherhood.

Maud

Maud had a mother who was extremely cruel, perhaps psychotic. For example, she used to take her dirty underpants and soak them in the soup. With Maud, there was a long series of terrible fights. When she hit puberty, Maud took to her bed for a week, not daring to say a word. Her mother declared her psychotic and had her hospitalized, but she was quickly released.

In therapy many years later, Maud revealed that her going to bed was quite voluntary; she knew exactly what she was doing. The only way out of her dilemma with her mother was a total retreat.

In the schizophrenic, this defensive device is known as catatonia, or sometimes a catatonic stupor. In such cases, the danger the person is escaping from is an imaginary terrorizing mother; in the case of Maud, however, it was her real mother.

Frequently a woman will adopt an attitude toward her own children that is the opposite of what her mother did to her. In the case of Pat, the actress discussed earlier in this chapter, the mother was exceedingly cruel; in her turn, Pat was totally indifferent, letting her children do whatever they wanted to do. Sylvia Brody and Sidney Axelrad, in their book *Mothers, Fathers and Children* (1978), argue that maternal neglect is one of the primary causes of neurosis.

Motherhood

Dorothy

The case of Dorothy shows another form of reaction against the mother. Dorothy was brought up under the most miserable of circumstances. She was born out of wedlock, and her father disappeared right away, never to reappear in her life. Her mother did the best she could and even got married, but she could not establish a good home for her daughter. Her marriage soon broke up, and she had to bring the child up herself. In the midst of numerous complaints about life and the burden that a child represented, Dorothy was brought up in dire poverty and misery.

In spite of this background, Dorothy succeeded in establishing herself as a professional in a free-lance field. She attracted a number of men and lived with a few. The major residual of her childhood was a total unwillingness to have a child. At one point, she became pregnant. The man involved wanted to marry her, but Dorothy would have none of it and chose to have an abortion. She remained with the fear of having a baby, in contrast to her mother who had had a baby illegitimately and spent the rest of her life regretting it.

We have passed in brief review a number of cases of motherhood. In some of these the woman is able to enjoy being a mother; in others she is not. Whether a woman will become one kind of mother or the other depends in part on the intimate relationships in her own family when she was a little girl.

At the same time, it can be argued that family circumstances have been overly stressed by feminists, who overlook the relatively simple tasks that the mother has to accomplish in order to bring up her child adequately. A lot depends on the child, too. The interaction between mother and child should be mutually gratifying. When it is, a healthy baby results, and later a healthy adult; when it is not, there is storm and strife.

Psychologists have contributed strongly to the recognition that there are many mothers who do not enjoy their children, and not merely because the child is "unenjoyable." Neglect is a primary concern of the clinician who is faced by a recalcitrant child. In such cases, she most often finds a mother who has neglected her child or made impossible demands on her.

6 | Separation from the Father

While the girl begins her life with her mother, it is always mother in the context of father—the dyad is part of a triad. Much has been written about the mother, yet the relationship with the father is also important. However, as R. Ekstein notes in his fascinating article, "Daughters and Lovers: Reflections on the Life Cycle of Father-Daughter Relationships," "The dynamic interaction with father has yet to be codified" (Ekstein, 1980, p. 207).

Even psychoanalytic theory has tended to bypass the father, concentrating for many years almost exclusively on the mother. Only recently has there been an effort to redress the balance (Fine, 1989).

Development of the Father-Daughter Relationship

Ekstein's outline of the way father-daughter relationships develop is quite useful. I shall summarize his main points here.

The father-daughter unity starts before the daughter's birth. It is as yet an undifferentiated unity, all in the mind of the father-to-be. Much of what he thinks now about the role of the daughter in his life depends, of course, on previous experience, on the quality of his marriage, on the existing conflicts in the marriage, and on the capacity of both mother and father to let the marriage dyad grow into a triad. It is a fantasy relationship, a fantasy that implies a psychic task, the capacity to develop trust for the kind of parenting that is required in a father-daughter relationship.

As a girl grows up, there comes a time when her father can no longer treat her as a little girl. Growth is different in different

Separation from the Father

girls, but generally speaking, the adolescent girl faces an intensive struggle as she tries to find her own identity and bring about a key step in the separation from her father. Free love, new marriage arrangements, and new means of birth control have driven adolescents into risks that they cannot master, and many of these risks come out in the crisis relationship that often exists between the adolescent girl and her father.

The daughter's relationship with the father is maintained if she succeeds in maturing to the point where she can give up her infantile bondage and create a new bond of love between herself and her father. Often, the father finds it difficult to let go of the daughter, particularly if other aspects of his life are unsatisfying. Father and daughter may enjoy each other on a different, higher level if she marries and has children; he will then become a grandfather and enjoy her offspring.

The picture given of the life cycle by Ekstein is a kind of model, a blueprint by means of which a father-daughter relationship can be better understood. The various points made by Ekstein are illustrated in the cases that follow.

Anna Freud

One case history that is well documented is that of Anna Freud, Sigmund's daughter. From an early age, Anna, Sigmund's sixth and final child, was his favorite. She went through school at the usual rate and soon became a teacher. Unlike all of Freud's other children, Anna identified with her father. As a consequence, she had a cool, indifferent attitude to men and never married. Indeed, it now appears that Freud rather actively dissuaded her from going out with several young men who might have been quite suitable, such as Ernest Jones. Instead, she lived with her friend Dorothy Burlingham from 1930 (when she was twenty-five) to the end of her life. Some have speculated that this was a homosexual relationship, but actually nothing intimate is known about it, and certainly there is nothing unusual about two women living with one another.

In 1923, Freud developed cancer of the jaw, the disease that was to kill him in 1939. During the intervening sixteen years, Anna felt called upon to be his constant nurse-companion, which further restricted her love life. Dynamically speaking, this was an Oedipal victory for Anna over her mother, who was said to be so well-preserved that she could still do her own shopping into her nineties.

When Freud moved to England in 1938, fleeing from the Nazis, Anna went with him, and they lived together in the same house in Maresfield Gardens. Freud died a year later, but Anna lived on in the same house another forty-four years. She kept his room preserved in exactly the manner that it existed at the time of his death, so that in effect she lived with her father all her life.

While Anna apparently never did develop sexually, in terms of a husband and children, she devoted her energies to her intellectual growth and the development of psychoanalysis, becoming one of the pioneers in child analysis.

Her choice of analysis as a profession was highly successful. She became one of the leading lights of psychoanalysis after Freud's death. Two of her books, *The Psychoanalysis of Children* and *The Ego and the Mechanisms of Defense,* are both classics that have enriched the history of psychoanalysis and are still valuable texts for the student today.

Karen Horney

It has often been argued that the theoretical views of psychoanalysts are influenced more by their own personal histories than by anything else. If we compare Anna Freud and Karen Horney, another great name in the history of psychoanalysis, this does indeed seem to be the case.

Born in 1885, Karen Horney was the daughter of a sea captain who frequently traveled and was thus away from home a great deal. He is described as stern, repressive and demanding; thus, the relationship between her and her father was the exact opposite of that between Anna Freud and her father.

Horney married an economist and had three children (one of whom became a Freudian psychoanalyst critical of her mother's views). In 1928 Horney wrote a paper stating, in effect, that a happy marriage was impossible, and indeed her own marriage later ended in divorce. Thus, Anna Freud could not marry because she was too

Separation from the Father

devoted to her father; Karen Horney could not make a happy marriage because she was in rebellion against her father.

While Horney is often praised as having built up a feminine psychology, that evaluation strays wide of the mark. She did not seem to appreciate the woman's need to become a mother and the gratification that many women receive from a loving man. Nor did she show any great appreciation of women's sexuality; for example, almost all the work on the importance of the clitoris has come in more recent years, following the work of Masters and Johnson in the sixties. After the early years, when she did write a number of good papers, she wrote five books for the public, disregarding her colleagues and their critical comments on her work entirely. She particularly ascribed neurotic conflicts to cultural conditions, but even this point was not fully developed and had been made by many others, including Freud himself.

Eve

Eve was the older of two children. Her father deserted the family when she was four but maintained an interest in his daughter, in contrast to his neglect of his son. Eve grew up with hero worship of prominent male figures, such as movie actors and the family physician, who was quite handsome. She slept in the same bed with her mother all through her adolescence, even though she frequently suffered from allergic rashes all over her body (she was allergic to grass).

In her adolescence Eve had various beaux, all of whom were considered inadequate by her mother. Eve's mother was extremely strict about any sign of sexuality. She would wait for Eve at the subway station when she came home on a date and escort her home, thus making it impossible for Eve to even kiss the boy.

When she was twenty, Eve met a young man who fell in love with her and proposed marriage. At this her mother became very angry, threatening to commit suicide if Eve went through with the marriage. Finally, after about two years of this, the marriage was permitted. It went well enough, except that at one time Eve had a winter of hysterical fits that made it impossible for her to go out on the street. Also, she remained a frightened, dependent woman all her life. For example, she worked for years as a substitute teacher but was always afraid to take the exam for regular teacher.

Elaine

Although a girl is supposed to love both parents equally, this often proves to be an impossible task, and the girl chooses one parent or the other (the Oedipal situation). As a rule, sexuality takes over and the girl prefers her father, while the boy prefers his mother, but there are many exceptions.

Elaine had a passionate involvement with both her father and her father's brother. Although she was just twenty-one at the time she came to therapy, there had already been a long series of men in her life. At one time she lived in Baltimore, where she used to go to burlesque shows and imagine herself as one of the strippers.

In order to make herself appear more glamorous, Elaine fabricated a story about her family. She said that the family had gone to Italy during World War II to do important war work, and that there she had met with an accident that crippled her slightly. None of this was true, but it sounded good. Elaine had told this story so often that she no longer knew to whom she had told it and to whom she had not.

In her childhood, Elaine had gone through a very passionate Oedipal period. On Sunday mornings she loved to get into bed with both parents and enjoy the feel of their bodies. These experiments had left such a lasting impression that she could still differentiate, in memory, the smell of her father from that of her mother.

Elaine's uncle Mike, her father's brother, was also a very significant figure in her life. He was a very demonstrative man who liked to play with his niece; he especially liked to tickle her. Nothing untoward ever occurred between them, but he became and remained an object of her daydreams.

When Elaine hit adolescence, she became overtly seductive toward her father, parading around in bra and underpants. However, he was a man who could not tolerate the slightest feeling of sexuality toward his daughter, nor could he bear to be close to her in any way. For example, when he had to go to the bathroom at night, he would get fully dressed, even to his shirt and tie, so that

Separation from the Father

no part of him could possibly be seen naked. During Elaine's adolescence he had a real breakdown, drinking excessively and ruining his business, which had to be taken over by Elaine's mother.

To curb her own overwhelming sexuality, Elaine married at twenty-two. Unfortunately she chose a husband who was as withdrawn as a man could be. Elaine reported that he could not dance and that sex with him was extremely brief and lacking in either foreplay or afterplay. He pursued a dry career as an accountant and, in marked contrast to his wife, never showed any sign of emotion or passion. In his background were a passive father and a paranoid mother, who always warned him against the dangers of life.

At first Elaine accepted her husband because he calmed her down. Eventually she became discontented with the status quo; at one point she even set her diaphragm on fire to signal her wish to have a baby. Before that could happen, she became attracted to another man, and soon she had left her husband and gone off to marry him. Their marriage, though stormy, was essentially a happy one. They had two children who grew up nicely.

In this case, Elaine first became enamored of her father and then acted out this desire with other men, finally, finding a man who was her equal sexually. Had she not been fortunate enough to find such a man, she undoubtedly would have drifted into worse neurotic difficulties.

Fanny

Fanny was the daughter of a high school teacher and a most puritanical man. Her father enforced the strictest code of conduct on her and her sister, who was two years younger. He made them dress in a prim-and-proper fashion, and they were not allowed to go out with boys until well into their teens; in addition, they were reprimanded for any sign of frivolity or sexual display. Fanny became afraid of her father, and this fear interfered with her relationships with boys.

Once she went to college, however, her father could not interfere with her escapades. Naturally, she was only allowed to go to a women's college, but she flirted as much as she could with the boys from a neighboring college. Her favorite sport was to go off on wild rides with several girlfriends, during which they would pick up boys and occasionally have sex with them.

What she did not yet know about her father was that he had an entirely separate life, in which he would seduce high school girls of the same approximate age as his daughters. He also had a long-standing mistress, unbeknownst to his wife. His repression of his daughters was obviously designed to curb his own sexual appetite for them, which he released by having sex with other girls their age.

In her twenties, unable to find a suitable field in which to work, Fanny married a much older man with whom she was not in love in order to have someone who would take care of her. Two children came of this marriage, a son whom she was wild about and a daughter to whom she was indifferent. The marriage was an unhappy one, and after a few years Fanny started an affair, which at least gave her some pleasure. She lived out her life in this way, never attaining much happiness but avoiding the most terrible misery.

Grace

When there is tension between a father and a daughter, the mother serves as a buffer. She can drive the daughter into the father's arms, or she can prevent the daughter from getting close to the father at all. In the numerous reports on the current scene of the rape and sexual seduction of young girls by their fathers, this buffering function of the mother is often forgotten.

When there is no mother at all, the conflict between father and daughter grows intense. A typical example is Grace, who was brought up in occupied Poland during World War II. The father, a physician, handed Grace over to a Catholic woman to take care of her while he went off and joined the partisans. When the war ended, he went to the woman to reclaim his daughter, but she refused to give Grace up. Typically for his aggressive character, he simply seized the girl and went off with her.

Grace's father took her to a displaced persons camp in southern Germany, where he slept in one bed with her with a pistol under his pillow. Grace was frightened out of her wits most of the time. She described her father as utterly relentless, even having sex with women while she was on the other side of the bed.

Separation from the Father

When Grace and her father came to America, they resided with various relatives. Grace's father wanted to regain his medical license; since his Polish accreditation was worthless in the United States, this was an awfully difficult task, but he persisted. Finally he was helped by an offer to go to Holland to complete his studies, which he accepted. He could not take Grace to Holland, so he placed her with a friendly woman in the United States. Grace did not know a secure home with her father until she was fifteen.

Once her home was established and Grace could go to school on a regular basis like other children, her father became openly sadistic. Obviously he was overstimulated by the closeness to his daughter, and, unable to take it out sexually, he became increasingly punitive. Grace lost track of the number of beatings he gave her.

Grace's father then tried to force his will on her by getting her to go to medical school, a vocational choice for which she had little sympathy and little aptitude. But he persisted, calling her a stupid little fool, interested only in boys and clothes. Her favorite hobby at that time was to buy movie magazines and read about the stars of the day. She was not permitted any dates in her adolescence; obviously, her father wanted to keep her to himself.

Grace did finally get to college, where she fell in love with one of her fellow students. As soon as her father heard about this, he went to the college and took her home. It is not surprising that she had a nervous breakdown at that point. She would sit for hours in front of the television set, daydreaming and barely able to move.

In order to get away from her father, Grace, after recovering from this breakdown, married at a very early age. However, she soon discovered that her husband was more interested in her money than in her. She had received a substantial sum of money from the German government as reparations for the loss of her mother. This she put in a joint account, and her husband withdrew it all from the bank. This enraged her to the point where she left him and went back to her father (largely because she had nowhere else to go).

Grace then found herself a clerical job that demanded little of her and lived at home for several years. During this period, her father constantly demeaned her, calling her stupid, boy crazy, and the like.

Grace's father by then had made several marriages, none of which lasted more than a few months. The mutual tie between father and daughter was so strong that neither could leave the other and make a normal marriage.

In spite of her maltreatment as a child and the continual contempt in which her father held her, Grace maintained her ties with her father. Although she married again and had two children, she could never calm down emotionally to make a happy marriage. Her father continued to abuse her verbally as long as he lived.

The Dyadic-Phallic Phase

Transitions are part of everybody's life, but they are especially prominent for women, who have biological markers that call for change (Mercer, Nichols, and Doyle, 1989). In a girl's early development, the transition from mother to father is especially important. This usually occurs prior to the Oedipal period. Greenspan (1982) has proposed a dyadic-phallic phase of development. During this stage, the father's role is unique in helping the child to stabilize basic ego functions such as reality testing, impulse regulation, mood stabilization, differentiation of self from others, and focused concentration.

An interesting addendum to this suggestion is the concept of "father hunger." When the father is present, he helps the children to reach ego resolution of various conflicts, as noted above. When the father is absent because of death or divorce, a striking feature of the children's psyches is the predominance of aggressive themes and content. This is especially noticeable in boys between the ages of eighteen months and sixty months. At a slightly later stage, between 60 months and 84 months of age, fatherless girls also begin to show strongly aggressive traits. These observations lead to the hypothesis that a specific role is played by the father in the modulation of aggressive drives in the young child, and the father's absence during the key period may have specific and long-range consequences.

A good illustration of the conflicts that can arise at this dyadic-phallic phase is the case of Harriet, a woman who later became schizophrenic. Harriet's mother was ill when she was born,

Separation from the Father

and she died when the child was one year old. Harriet was then brought up by her grandparents, who were already in their sixties. Her grandfather could not hear well and went around with an ear trumpet.

Harriet was obviously badly hurt by the death of her mother, but she also longed for her father, to whom she became very attached and who remarried when she was five years old. This remarriage left Harriet with a deep sense of rejection. Later she would say that she must be very peculiar since she was present at her own father's wedding.

When Harriet was nine years old, her father and stepmother moved to Puerto Rico, again leaving her in the care of her grandparents, who were now in their seventies. This increased her loneliness and eventually led to her being beaten by other girls. (Beating fantasies form an important topic in the psychoanalytic literature; Anna Freud wrote a classic paper on the subject.) For a number of years Harriet indulged in lesbian affairs in which she received beatings. When she was fifteen, she was sent to a school out of town where her homosexual activities became more pronounced.

When Harriet was twenty she became heterosexual, after which she got married. At first the marriage was a happy one, and twin girls were born. Faced with the demands of motherhood, Harriet began to fall apart and had an actual breakdown when the girls were a year old. The losses of her mother and father and the traumas of her girlhood proved to be too much for her fragile ego to tolerate. She was not hospitalized at this time but sought out a number of psychiatrists, none of whom was able to help her. After a number of these treatments, she attempted suicide by shooting herself with her father's gun, wounding herself only slightly. She was then hospitalized.

In this and subsequent hospitalizations she was given shock treatment of various kinds with little effect. Then she met and fell madly in love with a young psychiatrist. Apart from the fact that he came from a place near her home town, she knew little about him. He was actually a very disturbed man, the son of a judge, which encouraged him to see himself as a lawyer.

In the meantime, Harriet had been having trouble at home with her husband and daughters. When her husband went overseas during World War II, he fell in love with another woman. Harriet's psychiatrist took it upon himself to arrange the divorce, with all the necessary papers, since he regarded himself as a competent lawyer.

The divorce and remarriage of Harriet's husband precipitated another psychotic episode. This was handled by very intensive psychotherapy, in contrast to the previous episodes, which were handled by drugs and shock. This time the therapy helped her to establish herself in a more independent position. She was now a woman in her fifties; her children were grown up and had gone their own ways.

In Harriet's case, the remarriage and absence of her father subsequent to the death of her mother led to a psychotic resolution in her effort to find a mother and a father again.

The Passive Father

In the average American family today, the father plays an excessively passive role; "Mother knows best" is still the rule rather than the exception. It is this family structure that leads to the typical American neurosis: in the man, excessive passivity; in the woman, excessive frustration, depression, and hatred of the man. Some have argued that a change in child rearing practices in Eastern European countries, from a strict imposition of authority to a laissez-faire attitude, is responsible for some of the internal opposition that has sprung up against the stern communist regimes in those countries.

Irene was the daughter of a domineering mother and a passive, self-deprecating father. Her father had lost his business when he was still in his forties, and he reacted by becoming passive and self-condemning.

Irene was a bright student and did very well in high school, well enough to earn a scholarship to college. Her father, who had never been to college, discouraged her from going, saying, "From now on, everything's downhill." Her first reaction to this pessimistic, depressive attitude was to leave home and marry a young Irish sailor. It took her only a few months to recognize this as a serious mistake, and she sought out therapy to straighten out her life.

Irene went into therapy with a young, attractive psychiatrist,

Separation from the Father

with whom she promptly fell in love. Her marriage was now on the rocks, and the couple separated.

In the meantime, her father was getting steadily worse. He would smoke one cigarette after another in spite of all warnings, he would pace the floor all night, unable to sleep, and he would try to hold on to his daughter by asking for her sympathy, which she would not give him.

After her divorce, Irene began to experiment with other men. She took up with a black man from Nigeria, but when she discovered that he came of a polygamous tribe, she was flabbergasted and hurt. This led to a breakup of the relationship.

In a deep depression, Irene continued her experimentation with men. Throughout this period she always had in mind the image of her father, who had started so high in her estimation when she was a little girl and sunk so low when she was a grown woman. Disappointed in all the men with whom she had affairs, Irene soon began to fool around with women. When last heard from, she had reached bisexual resolution of her love life.

Every daughter wants to get a rise out of her father, especially in adolescence; usually this comes out most clearly in her sexual behavior. Irene wanted to get an appropriate response from her father, but he could not or would not give it to her. The same is true of Grace, Harriet, Fanny, and the other women discussed in this book. After the early experience with the mother, the father is the one who arouses the desires of the girl.

Untouchability

The need for a response is so deep that it may interfere with other functions. M. D. Davis and E. L. Kennedy (1990) show that a common role among lesbians has been the "stone butch," or untouchable butch, who does all the wooing (seeking a response) and does not ever allow her lover to reciprocate in kind. To be untouchable means to gain pleasure from giving pleasure. As Davis and Kennedy write:

> The archetypical lesbian couple of the 1940s and 1950s, the "stone butch" and the fem, poses one of the most tantalizing

puzzles of lesbian history and possibly of the history of sexuality in general. In a culture that viewed women as sexually passive, butches developed a position as sexual aggressor, a major component of which was untouchability. However, the giving of sexual pleasure was associated with the active or "masculine" partner, a service usually assumed to be feminine. Conversely the fem, although the more passive partner, demanded and received sexual pleasure and in this sense might be considered the more self-concerned, or even more "selfish" partner. These attributes of butch-fem sexual identity remove sexuality from the realm of the natural, challenging the notion that sexual performance is a function of biology and affirming the view that sexuality is socially constructed [p. 393].

Although these women drew on models in heterosexual society, they transformed the models into an authentically lesbian interaction. Through role playing they developed distinctive and fulfilling expressions of women's love for women.

When girls are brought up by a father who is indifferent to them, or by a father who punishes them severely for any infraction of the sexual rules, the untouchability issue becomes very important. Often, when these girls go into adolescence and begin to think about boys, the "untouchable" suddenly becomes the object of desire. This is the dynamic in much of the popularity of movie stars, who are actually objects on the screen, without real life to the teenagers who worship them.

Many of the men who are worshipped by teenagers are seriously ill, and some of them are quite psychotic. What is intriguing is that they attract so many girls, especially teenagers. One example is rock singer Elvis Presley, one of the highest-paid performers in the history of entertainment. He was born in Mississippi in 1935, an identical twin whose brother died in childbirth, leaving him an only child. His father was sentenced to jail in 1938 for forgery, leaving Elvis alone with his mother from the time he was thirty months until he was eleven. Without any formal training, Elvis learned whatever music he knew from the radio.

When he was sixteen, still living with his mother, Elvis went

Separation from the Father

through a series of nightmares. Night after night he imagined he was attacked by a mob of angry men. They would circle him continuously as he hurled defiant challenges. A violent struggle would ensue. Elvis would cry out in his sleep and toss about fiercely. Sometimes he would leap out of bed and whirl the sheets about his head. Sometimes he would be wakened violently by an agonizing jolt of pain as he smashed his fist into a wall or tore off a toenail kicking against the sheet. If he did not awake, he might arise from bed in a cold sweat, with eyes open but glazed, and make for the nearest door or window.

Such adolescent nightmares, in one form or another, are quite common. We would interpret them as a fear of his father's punishment for his incestuous wishes for his mother. It is striking that this man, later to be known as Elvis the Pelvis, who would excite millions of teenage girls, sexually never managed to have a normal life of his own. He was far too attached to his mother.

Soon Elvis began his professional career. As one of the most popular singers of his day, he earned (and spent) more than $100 million by the time he was forty. There is some mystery in these fabulous earnings. Elvis did not have an extraordinary voice; he was not an actor; he had no electric personality. What accounts for his success? Primarily, he became a symbol for teenage girls, the age on which he was fixated. Neither children nor full-grown women, teenage girls could identify with this man who likewise was not full-grown, but half boy and half man.

Elvis particularly liked a group of girls who would strip to their underpants and wrestle with each other while he watched. He accounted for the obsession by recalling an incident from childhood: a moment when he had seen two girls tumbling together on the ground with their dresses rising to show their crotches. Here are further instances of Elvis's untouchability; the girls could undress, in whole or in part, try to seduce him, *and not succeed.* This is the essence of the adolescent girl's sexual conflict with her father.

An interesting instance of the untouchability issue surfaced in the case of Holly. Holly was very angry at her father, for reasons that never became entirely clear. When she was a little girl and reached the Oedipal age, she began to have sex play for him (not with him). She would sneak around and grab his penis, at which time he would push her away gently. On other occasions she would suddenly pull down her underpants and expose herself, which did not get any reaction from him but a simple "Don't do that." Her later anger was in part a result of feeling that her sexual overtures in childhood had been rejected.

The Distant Father

While much has been written, especially recently, about fathers who are too seductive toward their daughters, the opposite, the silent, virtually nonexistent father, has been given too little attention.

Lydia, a twenty-three-year-old teacher, had a father who was virtually out of the picture. In his youth he had wanted to be an opera singer, but he abandoned this idea because he had neither the money nor the talent. He managed to eke out a living singing at bars and nightclubs. Then, at forty, he abandoned his ambition and married, which meant he had to have a steady job to support his wife and any children that came along. When Lydia was born, he took a night job to support the family—what is often called the graveyard shift. So he was seldom at home, nor could he ever spend much time with his daughter. He was the archetypical silent father, distant, uncommunicative, uninterested in his daughter's welfare or life.

Lydia resented this distance enormously but did not know what to do about it. Her early reactions were somatic—she developed rashes and illnesses of all kinds. She could not cling to her mother much because her mother was rather withdrawn and found it difficult to talk to people.

Lydia's sexuality began in the usual way but then turned toward a preoccupation with homosexuality. She joined women's groups and left home to live with a girlfriend. She was on the verge of becoming a complete homosexual when a friend told her about therapy. She consulted a psychiatrist, who referred her to another analyst, a handsome young man with whom she fell in love.

Lydia's therapy went smoothly until her therapist suddenly developed pneumonia and died. Lydia was devastated, but with the help of another therapist she was able to recover. Her love for the young man who died moved her toward men, which allowed her to

Separation from the Father

marry and have several children. However, her sexuality never fully developed. She could not have orgasms, and she actually resented any familiarity with her body. She particularly disliked the fact that her husband had a lot of body hair, just like her father. She could not enjoy her children and continually complained that she had never wanted to be a mother.

In this chapter we have examined the various difficulties a girl experiences in separating herself from her father and establishing an identity of her own. Only if she can successfully pass through the stage of being in love with her father will the girl become fully adult. In the next chapter, we will examine in more depth the woman who spends her entire life trying to please her father.

7 | The Entertainer

From time immemorial, woman has been seen as the stimulator of men, the one who brings him to life, both literally as a mother and figuratively as an attractive woman. In the Bible, Eve is the temptress who persuades Adam to eat from the tree of knowledge, which costs them both the Garden of Eden. A similar myth occurs among many people: the woman tempts man to enjoy himself; she is the source of what is most exciting and joyful in life. A Hopi legend goes as follows:

> Sotuknang went to the university wherein was Tokpella, the first world, and out of it he created her who was to remain on that earth and be his helper. Her name was Kokyangwait, Spider-Woman.
> When she awoke to life and received her name, she asked, "Why am I here?"
> "Look about you," answer Sotuknang. "Here is the earth we have created. It has shape and substance, direction and time, a beginning and an end. But there is no life upon it. We see no joyful movement. We hear no joyful sound. What is life without sound and movement? So you have been given the power to help us create this life. You have been given the knowledge, wisdom and love to bless all the things you create. That is why you are here."

Through the ages, and especially in the modern world, the woman has exercised her power in the form of the entertainer. The

The Entertainer

development of the girl proceeds from her mother to her father. The mother period is a relatively quiet one, in which the infant eats and sleeps. Then along comes the father, and the girl discovers that she can excite him—and thus play a new role in life, in which she is just as important to her father as her mother, if not more so. It is then that she wishes to become the entertainer, to excite him, to seduce him, to enjoy life with him.

As soon as she can run around, the little girl begins to be seen as a cute little creature, able to excite and entertain the grown-up man. It is no surprise, then, to find that women are frequently obsessed with entertainment. To have a schizoid man who retreats from women and the world is not unusual, but to have a schizoid woman who runs away from the world is rare.

Entertaining in childhood is associated with song and dance; in puberty, it quickly becomes associated with sexuality. A typical case is that of the music teacher Lucy (Chapter Four), which will be explored in greater depth here.

Lucy's father was the dominant figure in her family. He was born in Germany and came to the United States when he was grown up. Lucy remembered him as a handsome, aggressive man with a big moustache. He had a violent temper and would frequently get drunk. At such times he would sit in the living room throwing knives on the table and cursing loudly. This would scare all the children out of their wits. He was always threatening to leave home, though he never actually carried out the threat. He died when Lucy was nineteen.

Somehow everybody knew that Lucy's father had lots of mistresses. It was even rumored that he had had incest with his oldest daughter, Mary.

Lucy's mother was a quiet person who devoted herself to the traditional German "Kinder, Küche, Kirche" (children, kitchen, and church). She outlived her husband by some twenty years.

Lucy's first clear memory was from the age of five. She was all dressed up in her best clothes to go for a ride with her father. A picture was taken of them that she kept for a long time.

This and the next memory set a pattern for her life. One day her violin teacher induced her to open his fly and fondle his penis. She remembered quite well how much she enjoyed it. Her mother eventually found out about this and dismissed the teacher, but no legal action was taken against him.

When Lucy was nine, her brother-in-law, husband of the second-oldest sister, began to engage in sexual activities with her (he would perform cunnilingus on her). At first Lucy said she enjoyed it; later she said she was revolted by it. Her brother-in-law also took pictures of her, including a picture of her exposed vagina. These activities continued for about four years before they were discovered by Lucy's father, who threatened the brother-in-law with a beating if he ever came near Lucy again.

For the next several years, until she was fifteen, Lucy had no heterosexual experiences. However, she did have sex with a girlfriend a few times. Shortly after her fifteenth birthday, she embarked on an extremely promiscuous sexual pattern. She and her two sisters would march up and down a major avenue not far from her home and pick up men. As she later put it, she allowed the men to do anything they wanted to do with her. Usually they would take her somewhere and have intercourse with her.

Sex became Lucy's total obsession for a number of years. At school she could think of nothing else but whether she was pregnant. Twice she contracted gonorrhea, three times she had abortions. Her main fear, however, was that her father might discover what she was doing. Evidently he never did.

As she described herself in this period, she was the proverbial "easy lay," the girl who could not say no. Once one of Lucy's boyfriends brought along several friends who paid him for sex with her. Being turned into a prostitute proved too much for Lucy, and she called a halt to the relationship.

Around this time, Lucy fell madly in love. The boy showed some interest in her, but his family would not permit marriage. She never forgot him. Twenty-five years later when she accidentally heard something about him, it still aroused a strong warm feeling inside her.

Throughout this period, Lucy's schoolwork went steadily downhill, and there was a serious danger that she would flunk out of school. Her wish to become a concert violinist fell by the wayside. For a while she did leave school, but she came back to it later.

The Entertainer

At about the age of twenty, Lucy met her future husband. At one point before their marriage they had a fight and temporarily broke up. Lucy's fiance started an affair with a dance-hall girl, from whom he acquired syphilis. When the syphilis (which he had passed on to Lucy) was discovered, both were treated and completely cured. In that pre-penicillin era, the treatment involved a long series of injections in the buttocks that left scars. These "bumps," as Lucy called them, and the syphilis itself were a source of tremendous shame to Lucy—much more so, in fact, than her previous sexual activity.

Lucy's husband was an anxiety-ridden, passive man who had once attempted suicide. In their marriage Lucy assumed the dominant role. She was extremely erratic and moody, and he was compelled to put up with it. Constant fights were the order of the day. As soon as Lucy got a little ahead financially, she would refurbish the house, impoverishing herself all over again. Somehow she developed the ability to cry at will, and she used these hysterical outbursts to force compliance with her demands. She drank heavily, though never to the point where it interfered with her work.

At a later stage, psychotherapeutic help proved to be of considerable value; after all, Lucy was a classic hysterical personality, in some ways the personality most suited to psychotherapeutic treatment. Obediently she fell in love with her analyst and went through a regular transference neurosis. However, her husband's passivity became more than she could handle. Ideally it would no doubt have been best for her, after clarifying the history of her promiscuity, to leave her husband and strike out again on her own, but such a solution, defying conventional morality again, was beyond her. Besides, by this time there were children of whom she was very fond.

Lucy remained in the marriage even though she could never resolve all her problems there. In other aspects of her life, particularly her work as a musician, she did very well. At one point during her career as a performer she became terrified that the audience could look up her skirt when she was on the platform and see her underwear, but she was able to overcome this fear. All her life she remained attached to the entertaining and exhibitionistic sides of her personality.

The Need for Attention

Although she was often described as the sex symbol of her generation, Marilyn Monroe was a miserable woman. She was born to extreme poverty, and her mother was in a mental hospital for many years. Her father was killed in a motor accident. Throughout her childhood, she lived in one foster home after another.

According to some reports, Marilyn was as promiscuous as Lucy, though it should be noted that such stories are common about Hollywood starlets. She tried psychoanalysis with at least two top analysts, Marianne Kris and Ralph Greenson. Although Greenson even took her in to live with him for a while, neither succeeded in dispelling her terrible depressions. Marilyn tried suicide while in treatment with Greenson.

In 1949, early in her career, she posed for a nude calendar. At first the calendar did not sell, according to the photographer, but later it became her trademark, and every time a man looked at her he could think of her in the nude.

Although at one time she studied with the famous acting coach Lee Strasberg, Marilyn seemed to have little talent for acting. She made a small number of films, few of which seemed to have much artistic value, though some were very popular.

Marilyn married three times. An early marriage to Jim Dougherty was followed by two well-publicized marriages, to the baseball star Joe DiMaggio and to the playwright Arthur Miller. She had no children and led a rather rootless life.

Did Marilyn really have something special, or was she simply a woman who capitalized on the fact that she had posed nude at an early stage in her career? Nowadays, a nude picture is much less daring than it was in 1949. Did Marilyn really want to pose in the nude, or did she just stumble into it by accident? So many unanswered questions—and her analysts, who might have told us more, remained silent. Greenson even came to her defense once, posthumously—strange behavior for a psychoanalyst to deny the pathology in his patient.

To an analyst who does not know her, she looks and perhaps is schizophrenic—parading a lot of glitter with no real substance underneath. Traumatized as a child, she could never really get close

The Entertainer 91

to anyone. As one of her biographers, Maurice Zolotow, wrote, "Perhaps, for a great star of the combination of paradoxical and conflicting desires as Marilyn Monroe, there will never be, there can never be, an enduring love for another person" (1990, p. 359).

Marilyn Monroe presents what is typical of so many actresses—surface appeal and inner misery. She made the most of her surface appeal in her brief life and ended it in total misery. Truly she was typical of the actress who seeks instant acclaim, only to lose everything the next day. As her ex-husband Arthur Miller said of her in his play *After the Fall,* she had one word written on her forehead: *Now.*

A similar pattern of breakdowns emerges in the life of Carroll Baker (Baker, 1983). After the divorce that ended her unhappy first marriage (see Chapter Ten), an inevitable period of promiscuity followed. With the promiscuity came two breakdowns, which she describes in some detail. Both involved a return to her mother, a retreat from the rush and bustle of her sex life. About the first one she wrote, "It happened so suddenly. There must have been a void, a blackout, when or for how long I don't know. The first thing I remember was waking up in a nice cold bed. [Carroll had wet the bed when she was a little girl; this feeling could relate to that.] I was crying for you. I wanted my mother, but I didn't know how to contact you. I cried again and again, over and over again, but my cries simply circled the room and bounced right back at me. There must have been a telephone no more than an arm's length from my bed, but I no longer understood about telephones.

"I was terrified I couldn't see. There must have been a light switch nearby, an electric light bulb to illuminate my space—but I had forgotten such things exist" (Baker, 1983, p. 11).

It is clear that Carroll was becoming a little baby again. That is the psychological explanation of a "nervous breakdown," a lay term that has no exact professional equivalent.

The second breakdown occurred in 1966. Of this she writes, "What time is it? When did I take my last tranquilizers? I'm beginning to feel nervous. Maybe I should go to the kitchen and look at the clock. I'm too tired to move. I'll just sit here for a while."

This same pattern is seen in the lives of many other actresses: on the surface, glitter; underneath, sadness. It is essentially a manic-depressive pattern of a special type. In the manic swing the emphasis is all on how the actress appears to others; everything is sacrificed for momentary attention. This is the hallmark of the entertainer's psychology.

The progression begins to become familiar: a poverty-stricken childhood, a broken home, an absent father, early struggles—then an almost magical figure emerges out of the blue, the entertainer at her height—then sexual promiscuity, breakdown, and finally either sanity or more serious breakdowns leading possibly to suicide. Therapy is often resorted to somewhere along the line, but to the actress publicity is frequently more important then mental health, and therapy fails.

Child stars have always attracted a great deal of attention. Perhaps the best-known child star of this century is Shirley Temple, who rose to fame in the 1930s. Shirley's parents moved to Hollywood when she was only two, at which age she was already dancing. Shirley had begun to dance to please her mother, and she continued to dance to hold on to that love. She made rapid progress in the movies, dancing, singing, and acting like a charming little girl.

The Path to Maturity

For a number of years Shirley Temple was the leading child star of the day. She had played in fifty-six movies by the time she was fifteen, and often these were the most popular pictures of the day. She never went through a wild or promiscuous period. At sixteen she married because her mother had married at seventeen. The marriage broke up, and a year later she married again, a marriage that has lasted and brought her two children.

Shirley was unusual in the interest she displayed in serious affairs when she got older. From 1974 to 1976 she was ambassador to Ghana, while in 1981 she was a member of the U.S. delegation on African refugee problems, as well as a director of the National Wildlife Federation. The spectacle of an attractive woman as an ambassador to an out-of-the-way country like Ghana naturally attracted a lot of attention, and doubly so because she had been the most popular child movie star of her generation.

The Entertainer

In other words, attention and entertainment can be secured in many ways, and it is not necessary to gain it, as so many actresses do, by promiscuity, drinking, and wild reveling. Sally, for example, began to sing in her father's store when she was about three years old. Her singing was good enough to gather a crowd of customers around her. An uncle arranged a radio audition for her, after which she sang regularly on the radio. Her grandfather and family created a claque for her; they would regularly write fan letters to the studio after she sang.

As Sally grew up, she began to expand her entertainment to other outlets, with singing and dancing always remaining at the center of her activities. She began to get singing parts for adolescents, but an early marriage (at eighteen) stopped her theatrical career. She later returned to singing when her family was grown enough to allow her some leisure time. Again, it becomes clear that the wish for attention and the wish to entertain can be gratified in a number of different ways.

In fact, the one thing all actresses and other show people have in common is the wish to entertain; beyond that their personalities vary all over the lot. However, the case of Pat (Chapters Four and Five) is perhaps more typical than others. Pat was the younger of two sisters. Her older sister always took the initiative, so all through childhood Pat followed her around. With such a background, Pat grew up not knowing what she wanted to do in life. Her sister had become a doctor, but Pat could not imitate her because she did not do well in school. So after college, not knowing what else to do, she looked into acting. This appealed to her because all she had to do was follow the instructions of the director.

As an actress, Pat did not have much success because she was reluctant to make the rounds of producers, directors, and agents in search of work. However, she finally got a job as understudy to a prominent actress in a Broadway show. The cast went off to location in the Caribbean, where Pat had an affair with one of the show's stars. After that she went through a brief promiscuous period, having sex with all the men she could find.

At the end of this period, Pat felt very anxious and sought out therapy. The therapist was a young man toward whom she felt no great attraction, either positive or negative. Pat became increasingly interested in her understudy job, but she never got a chance to play the role on stage. After a few months, she had a breakdown and had to be hospitalized. Eventually she returned home and lived out her life there, isolated and unhappy.

There is no implication that all actresses are sick and promiscuous and should be hospitalized. It is merely pointed out as a not-uncommon pattern. In one famous case, an actor pleaded mental illness as a reason for not keeping a contract, arguing that mental illness is no handicap in an actor; he won the case, in that he was excused from the contract.

The actress Shirley Maclaine is a welcome exception to the rule. As she describes herself in her autobiography, *Don't Fall Off the Mountain* (1970, p. 42), "I was born into a cliche, loving, middle-class Virginia family. To be consistent with my background, I should have married an upstanding member of the community and had two or three strong-bodied children who ate Wonder Bread eight ways." Then came a little brother, Warren, who breathed the spirit of rebellion into both of them.

As a child, Shirley had some weaknesses in her legs. To correct this, she was sent to ballet class. However, in her first ballet performance she hurt herself and was hospitalized for four months. Later, after she recovered, she was bitten by the theatrical bug and moved to New York.

Her first years in New York were difficult, but in 1952 she got married, and two years later she landed her first good job, in *The Pajama Game.* Following that she was offered a movie contract in Hollywood. From there on, despite various legal difficulties, she went from one success to another.

Shirley's marriage was quite happy to all outward appearances. This started a round of gossip from the envious, seeking to undermine the marriage. Of the publicity she says (p. 113), "So much of an actor's life is played out in the newspapers. Many times actors are catalysts for people who don't speak directly to one another." She was unusual in that she explored the lives of the people whom she portrayed in her movies. For one movie she spent a great deal of time in Greenwich Village, getting to know the life of a broken-down Jewish woman. When she made *The Children's*

Hour, she spent hours with doctors discussing latent homosexuality in women.

Soon Shirley was making fabulous money and was world famous. What then? Other actresses have at this point taken a variety of lovers, resorted to drink or drugs, or hurt themselves in other ways. Not so Shirley. She studied. As she put it, "I reached for something more. I did it for survival, because I knew that to feed only on the rich food of my life would make me sick" (p. 2).

More interested in the people she played than in acting, she traveled very widely. Somehow she made this consistent with keeping a husband and bringing up a child. In India she became involved in yoga. The ultimate aim of yoga, her instructor said, is the liberation of the spirit, the union of the soul with the universe. Others might have tried psychoanalysis, but she had decided to experiment with her inner self in other ways. She kept on looking for new experiences: "My only emotion was the excitement of the unknown" (p. 225).

The year 1984 was a stunning year in Shirley's life. She won an Oscar for *Terms of Endearment,* triumphed in a record-breaking one-woman show on Broadway, and saw her provocative and brilliant book *Out on a Limb* become a nationwide best seller. With *Out on a Limb,* she resumed the spiritual journey she had begun in her early forties. This beginning became Shirley's doorway to the past. A crisis that nearly took her mother's life caused her to look at her parents' place in her life and in her heart. With the help of her spiritual guides, Shirley explored her choices, her beliefs, and her conflicts.

In her next book, *Dancing in the Light* (1985), she continued her explorations, this time discussing reincarnation, in which she had come to believe. In this book there is also a wonderful description of acting: "You [are expressing] the talent of giving and receiving, of resonating to a greater spirit by means of the body; the talent of souls appreciating one another, creating life on a larger scale. The talent of understanding the shadow awareness that makes us all one part of a divine perfection which is the essence of sharing. You are dancing with God."

This book too became a hit, no doubt because of her past and her personality. The idea of reincarnation, so basic to Indian philosophy, has never caught on with many Americans. However, Shirley's fascination with it has caught on because it is such an unusual quest for an actress and a modern American woman.

Shirley Maclaine's books about her personal quest form a kind of spiritual autobiography. As she put it, "I like to think of each of my books as a kind of map depicting where I've been and where I'm going. . . . In a series of expeditions to Africa, India, the Himalayan Kingdom, Bhutan and . . . Japan, I first reached out to touch the unknown and was changed by it. . . .

"All of this prepared me to return to a performing career with a greater enthusiasm and appreciation for the craft by which I earned my living and to explore what new levels of creativity I could bring to it. I believe the experience also helped to drive home another lesson. Anything is possible if you believe you deserve it." In an intimate journey inward, Shirley discovered the roots of her own existence and the infinite possibilities of life.

Whatever one may think of her philosophy, Shirley Maclaine is certainly a most extraordinary woman, far different from the average actress. Yet she is also an excellent actress, which shows once more that desires can be fitted into the most diverse outcomes and that someone who portrays other people to the world can also find herself in the process.

Lauren Bacall is another actress who succeeded in living a fairly normal life in spite of all the temptations of Hollywood. She sums up her life as follows:

> Statistically I fall into the broken-home category—brought up by one parent, my mother. Through pure luck—the luck of face and body, and having them noticed by others at the right time—I was given an opportunity to reach the highest of all highs at the age of nineteen. . . . With that I was also given a personal life fuller than I had ever dreamed I would have or, needless to say, have had since. . . . When it all went—though the career was more down than up almost immediately—why did I keep going? Why didn't I fall prey to the obvious pitfalls of life—booze, drugs, withdrawal? I would say that being loved unselfishly by two people had a hell of a lot to do with it. My mother gave to me constantly. And her support, her

The Entertainer

nurturing of me, her constant encouragement, together with the strength of our family and my own character—my ability to laugh at myself—all that is what made it possible for me to deal with Bogie, a man with three marriages in his past and twenty-five years on me.

And Bogie, with his great ability to love, never suppressing me, helping me to keep my values straight in a town where there are few, forcing my standards higher—again the stress on personal character, demonstrating the importance of the quality of life, the proper attitude toward work. . . .

I'm not ashamed of what I am—of how I pass through this life. What I am has given me the strength to do it. At my lowest ebb I have never contemplated suicide. I value what is here too much. I have a contribution to make" [1978, p. 23].

The story of Lauren Bacall's life can be told briefly. She was a child of poor Jewish parents; her father left when she was only six. She worked hard to get into the movies, but at first she was not very successful. However, when she got the chance to work in a film with Humphrey Bogart, her personal and professional lives merged and took off. She had only one love in her life—Bogart—and they were an idyllically happy couple. With two children, she led a healthy, wholesome life with Bogart; even though he died when she was still young (which was inevitable considering the differences in their ages), she idolized him, loved him, and enjoyed him to the very end. Again, she showed that being a famous actress did not have to interfere with the simpler pleasures of womanhood.

The life of Lucille Ball, who became a comedienne, was in marked contrast to that of Lauren Bacall. Lucy was born in a small town in upstate New York. Her parents' marriage broke up early. According to J. Morella and E. Z. Epstein's biography of Lucy (1990), a dominant influence in Lucy's life was a grandfather who took her to vaudeville shows. With the help of her stepfather, she broke into vaudeville early, and with considerable success. After these early exploits, she moved on from one show to another. Then she met Desi Arnaz, the scion of one of Cuba's wealthiest families, who had migrated to this country after Castro took over in Cuba. Their fighting served as the basis of a successful television comedy show, and Lucy became famous. However, according to Morella and Epstein, Desi Arnaz was addicted to liquor and womanizing. Lucy began having affairs as well. The excitement kept them going for years until at last the marriage broke up.

In sum, actresses come in many different sizes and shapes, both physically and psychologically. It is striking how often they come from broken homes. In the girl's upbringing, she moves to her father very quickly, with the wish to excite him and entertain him. This wish to entertain her father becomes the basis of her professional life, in which other men serve as a substitute for the father. The mother sometimes serves as a stabilizing anchor, sometimes not. There are many different outcomes to this scenario, but the central drama, the wish to entertain, and specifically the wish to entertain the father, is usually the same.

8 | Attachment and Loss

The early years of psychoanalysis were characterized by a strong emphasis on love and sexuality. The intact family, common in those days, was marred by excessive sexual repression and lack of love. Following the experiences of World War II, with its uprooting and murder of millions of people, the emphasis shifted to attachment and loss, which have remained among the main foci of psychoanalytic thought ever since. Thus by 1961, the psychoanalyst Engel could write that the loss of a loved person is as traumatic psychologically as being severely wounded or burned is physiologically. The experience of uncomplicated grief represents a manifest and gross departure from the dynamic state considered representative of health and well-being. It involves suffering and an impairment of the capacity to function, which may last for days, weeks or even months.

There can be no doubt that women, whose lives tend to center strongly on relationships, are much more involved with attachment and loss than men, though the role of attachment and loss in men's lives should not be underestimated.

Although Freud's paper on mourning and melancholia appeared in 1917, its full significance was not appreciated until much later. The work of Colin Parkes (1972) represents one of the pioneer efforts to examine the problem of bereavement. In terms of absolute numbers, there is evidence that more women than men succumb to disordered mourning. It appears, for example, that widows may be more prone than widowers to develop anxiety and severe depression. Men have learned to control their emotions, while women are given permission to express their grief reactions freely.

The English psychoanalyst John Bowlby has done the most extensive research on this topic; his findings are summarized in his three books on attachment, separation, and loss (1969-1980). The life cycle is often viewed as a series of separation-individuation experiences (Mahler, Pine, and Bergman, 1975); that is, a process of separating from loved ones and becoming ever more of an individual in one's own right.

Bowlby has espoused the view that mourning reactions in children are not necessarily different from those in adults. He distinguishes three stages in the reaction to loss: protest, despair, and detachment, with the last likely to be most pathogenic. However, Bowlby does not discuss differences in mourning between men and women.

Since the human being is an "attachment animal" and females are generally more attached than males, the subsequent loss of attachment bonds necessarily works harder on women than on men. In some monkey species, the infant literally clings to the body of the mother for six months or longer after birth (Harlow, 1974), which explains the basis of the human mother's strong attachment to her baby and to other people. Losses occur in any form of attachment—to people, to situations, to memories. The human life cycle is best understood as a long series of transitions that begin with separation and end with a reintegration into the social situation.

Desertion

The many troubles that women encounter in their lives can be grouped best under the kinds of losses that they experience. Death, desertion, sudden shifts in life situation (such as marriage), and birth make up the bulk of the therapeutic encounters that occur (Stroube and Stroube, 1987). Perhaps the most common problem for adult women is a sudden desertion by a husband or lover. These desertions cause a depression that is hard to overcome.

Jennie, an attractive pianist, was married to an analyst. They seemed to be getting along when one day he suddenly went off with another woman. Jennie fell into a deep depression, for which she was hospitalized, and she attempted suicide. She maintained her attachment to her ex-husband throughout her life, never really recovering from the desertion.

The abandonment left Jennie with a strong feeling of rage against all men, which prevented her from relating to other men. This anti-male feeling was so strong that she found a female doctor, a female lawyer, and a female analyst. No children had come out of the marriage, so her whole adult life came to center on her rage at her ex-husband. She was awarded a small alimony by the court, which she supplemented by working as a musician.

Jennie's ex-husband moved to Florida, where he established a practice and taught psychology at the local university. When Jennie found out that he was teaching a course in marital relationships, she was so angry that she got an article into the local paper revealing that her husband had deserted his own wife. He found out what she had done and applied to the court for a reduction in her alimony, which was granted for one year.

The ego ideal of the woman rarely responds favorably to her being portrayed as a deserted woman. Most women in this situation feel angry and vindictive, in addition to depressed. In Jennie's case, the vindictiveness took various pathological forms. At one point she developed the delusion that her mailbox lock was being picked by some prying stranger, which made little sense since there was nothing in her mailbox that would be of more than trivial interest to anybody. However, the thought made her feel important. Symbolically, it also represented the wish to have sex again with her ex-husband.

At one point, Jennie tried therapy with a male analyst, one who was fairly young and attractive. She would go only intermittently, and after each session she would send a long series of letters to the therapist, virtually reliving the entire therapeutic session and correcting or elaborating on many of her statements. It was obvious that the sessions excited her to the point that she could neither continue nor get over them.

Nellie was thirty, with two children, two and four years of age, when her husband left her to go off with another woman. She spent the rest of her life in a fury, never again relating to another man.

Nellie's background involved many losses. Her father had

died at thirty-six, when she was eight. Shortly thereafter, someone poisoned her dog, and it also died. When she was eighteen, she was surprised in her bath by a strange man who fled without doing anything, but the shock was intense. She married the first man who proposed to her, even though she was not in love with him. In school she did not go far; she was not exceptionally bright, and the academic material held little interest for her. She found work as a seamstress.

After the desertion by her husband, Nellie felt that her life was shattered. She had to go to work to support herself and her two children. In order to get along, she went to live with an older sister. Her work took up most of her time because her wages were low.

Nellie's relationship with her children became most pathological. The girl was forced to sleep in the same bed with her and never managed to grow up to be really independent. The boy was brought up to believe that his only purpose in life was to support her, and he rebelled against her strict domination in his teens by staying away from home as much as he could.

Toward her husband, Nellie's rage continued unabated. About ten years after he left, he began missing alimony payments; Nellie took him to court and had him jailed for three months for nonsupport. This she thought of as the greatest triumph of her life, and she never stopped telling her children that revenge is sweet. She discovered that her husband had entered the country illegally, so she reported him to the immigration authorities to have him deported; however, this tactic failed.

When a woman loses her man, she can either withdraw from the relationship or become vindictive toward the man. Both of these resolutions, if they can be called that, are seen in the above two cases. What the woman does not realize is that she loses sight of her own welfare by adopting the formula "revenge is sweet." The process of therapy will generally reverse or temper the rage and lead the woman back to paying more constructive attention to her own life.

Thelma, a hospital employee, was going steady with a Japanese boyfriend. One day he announced that he was leaving her and also leaving his job; he gave no reason, but she sensed that he was going off with another woman.

Even in therapy Thelma was inconsolable. Why did he do it?

Attachment and Loss

She did not even inquire more deeply into the relationship, just repeated almost mechanically, "Why did he do it?" After a few sessions she left therapy, left her job, and left her home. Short of suicide or psychosis, this is the most extreme reaction seen.

Loss

Reactions to losses can take many different forms; there is no one universal pattern, but a dynamic interconnection between the loss and the subsequent reaction can generally be drawn.

Mabel was vacationing in a country resort with her two children, a girl of five and a boy of three. The boy was warned to stay away from the road, which at times was heavily traveled. He would not obey, and one day he was killed by a passing car.

Mabel's reaction could scarcely have been predicted. She went into a promiscuous period, sleeping with virtually every man she could find in an effort to get pregnant again. Her husband objected rather strenuously, and they separated, but she continued her almost indiscriminate search for another child. Eventually she did find another man, got married, and had two more children, but the strain on her life was tremendous. She became terribly obese and died at an early age.

By contrast, the reaction of Evelyn, a thirty-year-old teacher and housewife, was easier to understand. Evelyn was in love with her family physician. He was a rather poorly trained person who turned to gynecology as he got older because it was a more stable practice than that of a general practitioner. Evelyn remained with him for the birth of her second child. Unfortunately, he bungled the procedure, and the baby died in childbirth.

Evelyn, though distraught, was seemingly under control. She went to another, more experienced physician for her third pregnancy, and the baby was born without any problem. However, the toll taken by the death of the second child in childbirth could not be shaken off so easily. After the birth of her third child, Evelyn went into a severe hysterical state, crying, shaking, unable to eat, angry at everybody. Fortunately, she responded well to psychotherapy.

A rather unusual identification occurred in another of my

patients, Miriam. During one of her sessions, my wife went into labor, and I took her to the hospital. At the time Miriam didn't show any reaction to the interruption of her session. Several years later, Miriam, by now married, became pregnant. About 8 P.M. her water broke. She called her physician, but he evidently did not want to be bothered and told her to call him in the morning. When she came to her therapy group that evening, the other group members urged her to go to the hospital immediately since it was dangerous to have a dry birth. She complied, and the baby was born about 3 A.M. At the end of all this, Miriam came away with the conviction that my baby was born during her analytic hour and that her baby was practically born in my office—an obvious distortion of her own wish to have a baby by me.

Fear of Loss

Many times the fear of some catastrophe can be as traumatic as the catastrophe proper. Linda exemplifies a problem of this kind. She was afraid of pregnancy but nevertheless married and had one child, a boy. Then she began to withdraw from sex in order to avoid having more children. This led to the fear that she could get pregnant through any kind of encounter. She convinced herself that sperm were so powerful they could get into her whenever she was nude or scantily dressed. Specifically, this first took the form of avoiding swimming pools because she thought that the towels used by men carried semen and could impregnate her. From this her fears of pregnancy expanded to embrace many different situations.

Linda avoided any kind of intimacy with her husband for fear that it might make her pregnant. Her gynecologist prescribed several contraceptives for her, but she would not believe that they were safe. Finally she went into therapy. Here she made some progress at first and became interested in sex again. In order to find out more about sex, she bought a well-known marriage manual. On one page the author discusses the penetrating capacity of the sperm and states that there are cases known in which a girl, sleeping in the same bed with her brother, became pregnant after her brother ejaculated. This story created a panic reaction in Linda.

Linda had had a hard time during the delivery of her child.

Attachment and Loss

It was obvious that the fear of another pregnancy and a difficult birth was all-powerful in her mind. It took hard therapeutic work to get her over this fear.

Ruth was the older sister in a very strangely organized family. Her father, a carpenter, had been born in Europe and had little familiarity with American ways. He married a woman twenty years younger, and they had two children. But trouble soon intervened, and the couple separated, although they continued to live in the same house. The younger sister slept in the same bed with her mother all through her childhood; Ruth slept in her father's bed.

This was all tolerable until Ruth began to menstruate. Her mother would not give her any tampons or sanitary napkins but insisted that she use toilet paper. Ruth did so until one day in school the toilet paper fell out and she dripped blood over the floor, to her terrible humiliation. Other problems followed.

Then Ruth decided that father, in whose bed she still slept, was going to rape her. To avoid that she went to another part of the house to sleep. Her sister continued to sleep with her mother. Apparently nobody inquired what Ruth was doing; in such a family, there is no real communication.

Ruth was thoroughly bewildered by the turn of events in her adolescence. She had nobody to talk to. In her despair, she thought of jumping off a bridge, then changed her mind and went to Bellevue (the chief hospital in New York for ambulatory schizophrenia). At Bellevue, she was assigned to a young, handsome psychiatrist, with whom she entered therapy. As she related it later, however, all that she did in therapy was observe his crotch.

Upon graduation from high school, which was as far as she wanted to go, Ruth saw an ad in the newspaper for dancers. It was actually an ad for girls for a burlesque show, but she did not know it. Many of the girls in the burlesque show were prostitutes, and Ruth got her first real education in the ways of the world. Men propositioned her, but she was wise enough to reject all offers, which were essentially fee-for-sexual-favors offers. Then a big battle with one of the other girls erupted, and Ruth decided to return home.

Ruth had almost no skills, so she took a series of jobs as a typist-clerk. Usually she would be fired from the job after a short time because of her uncooperative attitude. For example, if the boss told her that there were no more coffee breaks, promptly at 10 A.M. she would go over to him and announce that she was going out for a cup of coffee.

In her love life Ruth also drifted from one man to another without fully knowing what was happening. One of her therapists tried to seduce her; Ruth liked the attention but was smart enough to know that that sort of thing could not lead to anything good for her.

Eventually Ruth met a prominent poet in his forties, who fell in love with her and wrote poems about their sexual experiences. He was of about the same age as her father, so she settled down to live with him. Her father died, her mother and sister went off to Israel, and she stayed on with her lover, perhaps as good a resolution as a girl in her position could find (she was then only twenty-two).

Separation and Individuation

In the early days of psychoanalysis, the emphasis was on traumatic experiences, and the therapeutic process consisted of a search for those traumas in childhood. Much has changed since. Today the essential emphasis is on rejection by other people or reaction to the losses that have taken place in the person's life. The formula is separation-individuation for everybody, but for the disturbed, the separations are far harder to handle than for the undisturbed.

An excellent example is the life of Sylvia Plath, an American poet who died of suicide at the age of thirty. Her father was a professor of German who married one of his students, they had two children. Sylvia was a promising young poet, graduating from Smith College with high honors and an appointment to teach there. However, suicide filled her mind from an early age, and she kept on toying with the idea until she actually did it. At one point she read Freud's *Mourning and Melancholia* and wrote that it was "an almost exact description of my feelings and reasons for suicide: a transferred murderous impulse from my mother unto myself: the 'vampire' metaphor Freud uses, 'draining the ego' that is exactly the feeling I have getting in the way of my writing. Mother's clutch. I mask my self-abasement (a transferred hate of her) and weave it with my own real dissatisfactions in myself until it becomes very difficult to distinguish what is really bogus criticism from what is really a changeable liability" (Stevenson, 1989, p. 147).

The mythology that grew up around Plath after her death has obscured her serious pathology. In childhood she was the family darling, attached to her professor father and her housewife mother. At the age of seven, she wrote a revealing poem

> When mother goes away from me
> I miss her as much, as much can be
> And when I go away from mother
> She misses me and so does father.

This poem brings out her intense loneliness and difficulty in leaving her mother, already evident at that age.

Plath achieved a good deal in her life. She wrote, was well published, taught, married, and had two children. Yet the inner demons of attachment and loss were too much for her. Eileen Simpson, the ex-wife of the poet John Berryman, wrote a book about the poets she knew, the motto of which was taken from Wordsworth: "We poets in our youth begin in gladness;/But thereof comes in the end despondency and madness." So it was with Sylvia Plath.

Sylvia Plath tried several bouts of psychotherapy but never succeeded at it. Like many writers and other artists, success was more important to her than inner peace and calm. Indeed, many artists become opposed to therapy because they fear, erroneously, that it will deprive them of their gifts.

The manic-depressive life that Sylvia Plath led has been well described by her biographer, Ann Stevenson, who calls her book *Bitter Fame* (1989) and titles the first chapter "The Girl Who Wanted to Be God." The difference between Sylvia Plath and normal neurotics is that she was able to put her emotions into very expressive phraseology, whereas the average person just suffers or acts out in drink, drugs, or some other form of escape. This is not to be understood as meaning that all artists are neurotic; quite the opposite is true. Artists have creative impulses that they learn to express in a form that is meaningful to others. However, the torment that is attached to these inner impulses is frequently something they do not want to try to understand, which is why their therapy is so often unsuccessful.

Freud and others have described the manic-depressive alteration (much gladness in youth, much despondency in age) for many other well-known artistic personalities, such as F. Scott Fitzgerald, Thomas de Quincey, and Dylan Thomas. It is also a personality type often seen in ordinary life.

Ellen was so cheerful in her adolescence that she was known in her father's publishing firm as "the little sun." Then, shortly before she graduated from high school, she was stricken with juvenile diabetes, which determined the course of the rest of her life.

The first consequence of her diabetes in her life was that she had an affair with a much older man. He liked to keep his penis inside her all night (attachment), which made her feel warm and comfortable. When her father found out about this affair, he threatened to have her lover dismissed from his employment, and this led the man to break off the affair.

Then Ellen fell deeply in love with a man her own age. At first this affair looked like a happy and suitable one; the only trouble was that Ellen had to give up her schooling and live entirely through her husband.

Juvenile diabetes is not an easy illness to live with. Manic-depressive mood swings are common in sufferers from the illness. In Ellen's case, depression followed the recognition that she could not get pregnant and therefore would never become a mother. This was followed by a suicide attempt.

As time went on, Ellen became increasingly attached to her physician, who was of about the same age as her father. He was a rather troubled man, irritated with his patients and often chasing them away by pooh-poohing their complaints (he was an internist). Eventually she left her husband and married her physician, in spite of the diversity in their ages. Her parents were so angry at this that they would not come to the wedding.

The second marriage was one of constant togetherness, which many people mistake for love. Actually, togetherness of this kind is more often than not merely a cover-up for loneliness. Ellen's husband had left his wife, who was a much older woman, and

Attachment and Loss 109

abandoned much of his practice so that he could spend as much time as possible with Ellen. In spite of that, Ellen became steadily more depressed; again the demons of childhood had her in their grip. Her diabetes became increasingly difficult to handle, which is the nature of the illness. In her early forties she lost sight in one eye, again a common result of her illness. Therapy was tried, but she would not persist and quit after a few sessions. At forty-four, she tried suicide again, and this time she succeeded.

Ellen was not a poet; in fact, she had no artistic outlets, so her life course can only be described in psychiatric terms. However, her life was in its essence very similar to Sylvia Plath's, just less dramatic. Since she was not well-known, it was a life that attracted no one's attention outside of her family. Yet the dynamics were similar—mood swings from high to low, ecstatic to depressed; sunny in childhood, gloomy in adulthood. This pattern is repeated in many women.

Psychiatry has been under strong attack in recent years. J. Robitscher, who was a psychiatrist, psychoanalyst, and lawyer, argued that psychiatry is a form of social control, not of medicine. In lawsuits against the International Psychoanalytical Association and the American Psychoanalytic Association, psychologists have been victorious in eliminating the medical monopoly on psychoanalysis. In California, psychologists have gained the right to admit patients to hospitals and discharge them without medical supervision. In Hawaii, psychologists have gained the right to prescribe various psychotropic drugs.

In the face of these changes, many questions have been raised about the accuracy and meaning of psychiatric diagnosis. The ideological basis of psychiatric diagnosis is that the psychotic is irrational. However, this explanation does not account for despotic rulers like Stalin, Hitler, and now Saddam Hussein, who are quite rational but full of hatred for people. It would be more sensible to order psychiatric diagnoses around hatred rather than reason. After all, many people are irrational and quite harmless. What is the purpose of putting these people away or giving them drugs?

If hatred is made the basis of a diagnosis of psychosis, then the cases can be sorted out on the basis of the direction and intensity of the hatred. Then we could have a mother psychosis as well as a father psychosis.

Such intense father hatred came out in the case of Olga, a thirty-year-old woman who was drifting through life. She was the daughter of two general practitioners, neither of whom had time for her as she was growing up. She was not really attached to either parent but vented her spleen on her father, who was quite friendly and supportive of her; even in her late twenties, he was supporting her in full.

This hatred prevented Olga from acting constructively to further her own career. She did get through college, but then her father, who had been feuding with her mother all her life, divorced and remarried. This led to an almost uncontrollable fury in Olga. Her father sent her to analysts, but she would go once or twice, then quit with the repetitive complaint that it was not her but her father who needed treatment. Her demand that her father should be analyzed was eventually granted, but that did not calm her down. It was never very clear what she wanted her father to do; all that she apparently wanted out of life was to vent her spleen on him.

Olga's father was desperate to help her, but every effort was repulsed. Every time Olga saw him, she would fly into a diatribe against him that had neither rhyme nor reason. It was like the rages of the little girl before the temper tantrum period comes to an end.

Olga ended her therapy still in this state—unable to do anything about herself and taking it all out on her father. Again, as with Sylvia Plath, the demons of childhood persisted; Olga had felt rejected by both parents, and the sense of rejection never went away.

Death

Another experience that usually has severe repercussions is the death of someone close, no matter what the age. As noted before, Bowlby and others have shown that the child goes through a deep mourning process just like the adult.

In the case of Pamela, a fifty-four-year-old woman who was seemingly happily married, the death of her father aroused a tremendous reaction. Her father, to whom she was very attached, was in his eighties, so it came as no great surprise when he succumbed to a heart attack one day. The surprise was her reaction. On the surface she showed no emotion, but underneath she resorted to some

Attachment and Loss

foolish actions. Without rhyme or reason, she gave up her marriage to a kind, well-established physician who had always treated her very well and began a series of affairs with other men that became the talk of the town. She aged measurably, without any noticeable cause, and six months after his death she looked twenty years older. Her grandson was accused of molesting other boys sexually, and she became involved in a long legal battle for his defense. Her arthritis worsened to the point that she had to walk with a cane and required other supportive services. She never remarried and lived alone with the memories of father. Within ten years she was dead, evidently unconsciously longing to join her beloved father.

A different kind of attachment-loss pattern was seen in Olivia (Chapter Four), a twenty-four-year-old unmarried woman. Olivia had a younger brother who was suddenly stabbed to death by another young man in what was diagnosed as a homosexual revenge; before his death, few had realized that the boy was homosexual. Olivia reacted by an intensification of her own promiscuous wishes and several troubling neurotic traits, such as pulling out her hair and sucking on it.

Olivia had had a serious accident at age seven that left her with the appearance of being mentally retarded, although she was not. Seemingly, she had few talents, but she was interested in art. Although she worked as a typist, she began to pursue an artistic career. No one had ever evaluated her as being artistically gifted, but the wish to make art was strong in her, and she persisted. Eventually she became a fairly good artist and had several one-person shows.

Artistic reaction to a childhood loss has been noted by many; the art is a way of overcoming the disappointment of childhood. Leonardo da Vinci, for example, was taken from his mother by his father when he was not yet five years old, and the rest of his life was spent looking for an appropriate mother figure. The famous Mona Lisa painting is considered part of his search for a mother (Freud, 1963–1974).

Fantasy Versus Reality

Wanda, a beautiful thirty-year-old redhead, lived with her mother and sister in a two-story house in Brooklyn. She slept in the basement, separate from the others. One night she heard, or thought she heard, the doors open and a man walk in; the man then disappeared. She was so frightened that she sought out a psychiatrist attached to the school system in which she worked. This man first elicited the fact that she was a virgin. Then he said, in reference to her fears, "I will hypnotize you and take that away from you." In her own mind, Wanda was not sure whether he meant to take away her fears or her virginity. In any case, she decided to seek help elsewhere.

One of the main factors that came out in her later therapy was her strong reaction to the death of her father when she was ten and to an attempted seduction by an older cousin when she was thirteen. As she told about the attempted seduction it became obvious that she was quite a willing participant. If she was alone in the house, which happened often enough, her cousin would stop by, and she would let him in and allow him to fondle her breasts, which were just beginning to grow. Naturally, Wanda was afraid to tell her mother about this.

Wanda frequently went to nearby resort hotels, where she would be approached by literally dozens of young men. She would give them her number and say something like "Call me Tuesday at 7 P.M." If the man did not stick to the letter of her invitation but called her, say, at 7:15 P.M., she would hang up on him immediately.

In therapy she displayed extreme suspiciousness. For example, even though the therapist was seeing her for a minimal fee, she would demand a receipt, which was unusual, and explain that she was afraid that when she came back the next week the therapist would claim that she had not paid him. At one stage she developed an itch in her anus; when referred to a gynecologist (a woman), she would not undress, demanding instead that she be given an immediate explanation.

It was never really established whether a man had entered Wanda's room or not; the particulars she gave were very vague. She dated very frequently, and her dates usually ended up in a fight with the man for not valuing her enough. Eventually, however, she managed to find a man she felt she could be happy with, and she married and left the city. No follow-up was possible.

Many of the problems encountered by psychoanalysts are hard for the lay person to understand because so many people are responding to their internal fantasies rather than to external reality. The more disturbed such people are, the more they rely on these

Attachment and Loss

internal fantasies, and the further they get from external reality. The above case is a good example. Did the door open? Was there a man there? Or was it all the fantasy of a thirty-year-old virgin?

Masochistic pleasure, so hard to grasp, is a good example of this problem. Pearl, a clerk, complained that her boss was always staring at her. She worked in a stenographic pool in which there were a number of clerks. When asked to draw a picture of her boss's office and its spatial relationship to her desk, it became apparent that he could not even see her from where he was sitting; she was just giving voice to her imagination.

In an interesting recent paper by Anita Katz on the paradoxes of masochism, she told the following story (Katz, 1990, p. 237):

> A patient was told by her parents at the age of five that they were taking her for ice cream. She was brought to the hospital and the last thing she remembers is the mask being put over her face prior to a tonsillectomy. . . . This woman has recounted numerous episodes from childhood in which the promise or expectation of fulfillment has been associated with being sadistically tricked by others. This remains an important resistance in her analysis as well as a roadblock against expansive following through in other relationships, in libidinal pleasure, or creative fulfillment. The anticipation of an endeavor or relationship leading to fulfillment, pleasure or joy, is accompanied by the dread of being invaded tyrannically, ripped open mercilessly and exposed and picked on to the point of devastation.

This process in the masochistic individual is similar to the manic-depressive swings noted before; it is understood as a manic-depressive swing in relation to an internalized object or person rather than to a real event.

In sum, the attachment-loss model explains much of what happens with human beings. Many examples have been presented in this chapter, and many others come out in cases described in other chapters. This separation-individuation paradigm has become a major source of thought and theory in modern psychology.

9 | The Single Woman

All societies are organized around marriage. As a consequence, single women have historically been rather rare—and rather ashamed of themselves when they do exist. While the women's liberation movement, taking off from Betty Friedan's book *The Feminine Mystique* (1963), has tried to downplay the value of marriage for women, feminists have actually made little dent in the woman's wish for marriage. The great majority of women still marry, and almost all prepare for marriage throughout their younger years.

The great change is that women now also prepare for work. Today it is just as important for a woman to have a career as it is for a man. Yet in seeking to find happiness in work, women encounter many problems. Men have always complained about the burdens of work: the hours are too long, the demands are too great, the rewards are too small (the term "wage slave" was coined in the nineteenth century). Women are now discovering the salience of these observations. Many want to go back to the emotional and financial security of the traditional family, although it should be said, in all fairness, that many do not. The situation thus becomes confused for the modern woman, and as it becomes confused suffering enters the picture. The economic burdens that have been borne by men for centuries have now shifted to women, and they do not enjoy them.

Sylvia Hewlett, an economist who has researched the problems of women more thoroughly than anyone else, presents some significant statistics on the wage gap between men and women (1986). Only 7 percent of employed women in America work in managerial positions, and only 10 percent earn more than $20,000 a year. Three-quarters of American working women continue to be employed in traditional "women's jobs" and spend their time waiting on tables, typing letters, cutting hair, emptying bedpans, and cleaning offices. Most are badly paid. In 1984, one out of every four women earned less than $10,000 a year when working full time. In many cases, women's salaries fail to lift them above the poverty line, and this produces much hardship in an age when women's wages are essential for living, not simply pin money. Thirty-five percent of single mothers fall below the poverty line.

The wage gap (the difference between men's wages and women's) continues to be a burden. In 1939, women earned 63 cents to a man's dollar. In 1985 they earned 64 cents to a man's dollar, obviously not much change in fifty years.

In 1984, the median earnings of women who worked full time year-round was $14,479, while similarly employed men earned $23,218. A woman with four years of college still earns less than a male high school dropout.

In almost every occupation, men's salaries are higher than women's. Male lawyers between the ages of twenty-five and thirty-four earn, on average, $27,563 a year; the figure for female lawyers is $20,573. Bus drivers average $15,611 if they are men, $9,903 if they are women. In retail work, men average $13,002 a year, while women average $7,479 a year. Hewlett comments that we seem to have eliminated sexist terminology without doing anything about economic inequality.

The wage gap lasts into old age. There are sixteen million women over sixty-five years old in the population. In 1982 their median income was $5,365, compared to $9,188 for men. The main reason for the disparity between the incomes of elderly men and women is that the jobs women hold are rarely good enough to qualify them for private pensions, and only 11 percent of women over sixty-five collect pensions. It seems plausible that more older women than older men are supported by their grown children, but statistics are not available on that.

Perhaps the biggest surprise is that elite women are not closing the economic gender gap. Census data show that more women hold executive and professional positions than ever before—the percentage of managerial jobs held by women rose from 14.5 percent in 1960 to 28.9 percent in 1980—yet over those two decades the wage gap between men and women executives actually widened.

To end the wage gap, the principle of comparable worth, meaning equal pay for equal work, has been set up as a guideline. Perhaps the most important legal decision on this question came in 1983 when a federal judge ordered the state of Washington to pay its women workers $800 million in back pay wage increases on the basis of a comparable worth evaluation.

Women often find that family responsibilities interfere with advancement up the corporate ladder. Men find the same thing but are more willing to sacrifice their personal satisfactions for the sake of occupational or professional success. Nevertheless, women have entered the world of work, creating one of the great transformations of the twentieth century (Fine, 1990b). Sylvia Hewlett sums up the economic plight of modern women as follows:

> Accompanying the breakdown of traditional marriage in the late Sixties and Seventies was a dramatic rise in the proportion of women who work. This was part cause, part consequence. The weakening of traditional roles forced women into the labor force, while the fact of working and earning salaries enabled more women to free themselves of the bonds of traditional role playing. . . . Our mothers sought and the majority of them found security in marriage, but that avenue no longer offers any such guarantee. Because of stagflation, higher rates of unemployment and much higher rates of divorce, men can no longer be relied on to be family breadwinners—at least not over the long haul. The escalating divorce rate is a critical factor because with divorce men generally relinquish responsibility for their wives and often for their children. Thus the breakdown of marriage massively increases the disparity between male and female incomes [Hewlett, 1986].

Love and Work

The psychology of a woman centers not only on her love life—her desire for marriage with its companionship and sexual gratifica-

The Single Woman

tion—but also on her newly found work life. The case histories of single women that we shall discuss next reflect this dual problem of love and work (Fine, 1990b).

Mona

Mona was her parents' darling. This was both a blessing and a handicap, since she would never receive so much love and affection from a man. As a child, she was rather sickly, and her mother for a while had to feed her by hand, spoonful after spoonful. This she did faithfully, creating a dependency conflict in Mona that she could never overcome.

As Mona grew up, she remained rather passive, hoping for a great deal of love from teachers, friends, and relatives. The result was that she remained at home for an extremely long time, until well past thirty, and could not launch herself into the outer world.

One of her most powerful memories was of worry about her father. When he was asleep, she would put her head on his chest to see if she could hear his heart beating. Obviously there was a considerable amount of ambivalence about him, of which she recognized only the positive feelings.

Mona was a cheerful, outgoing girl whose main stumbling block, in the traditional family in which she grew up, was sex. Her parents loved her very much, but when she reached adolescence she had to be a "good girl." She could not take boys to her room, she could not stay out too late, and she had to suffer many other old-fashioned restrictions. The net result was that she had to be a stay-at-home and did not develop in adolescence a relationship that led to marriage.

In her work, she naturally gravitated to nursery school teaching, where she did quite well, moving up the ladder quite consistently until she was managing a nursery school herself. At the same time, she introduced a number of innovations in teaching that made her nursery school especially attractive.

However, her love life lagged behind because of her earlier prudish upbringing. While she succeeded in various relationships with men, she would primarily attach herself to older married men who half-promised to leave their wives and marry her but never did so.

In her sex life, Mona began to go in for sado-masochistic practices, particularly allowing herself to be beaten. She went on in this way for years, satisfied in her work life, frustrated in her love life, taking it out in beatings.

Nadia

Nadia began as a secretary to the president of a publishing company and worked her way up to becoming his valued assistant. However, at home, as the youngest of three children, she had to take a back seat to a domineering older brother. This inhibited her love life to such an extent that she could never form a mutually gratifying relationship with a man. At one point in her forties, she went out on many dates, but they did not satisfy her, primarily because she remained sexually frigid. This sexual experimentation could not make up for the earlier years of refusal and frustration. Nadia rationalized her plight by saying that she was pursuing an "alternative life-style," but inwardly she continued to feel lonely and frustrated. If the libidinal release comes too late in the woman's life, as here, it does not succeed in its effort to make her happier. Nadia was not markedly unhappy or neurotic, but she could find little joy in anything outside her work.

Antonia

Antonia, a forty-five-year-old schoolteacher, experienced difficulties in her life that were quite common in women before the sexual revolution of the second half of this century. She was the child of a very poor family, one of four sisters brought up to be dutiful daughters. The first problem that she remembered facing in her life came when she developed hair lice ("nits") that resulted from the lack of hygiene in her home. She was sent home from school, and eventually the lice disappeared.

Antonia's father had never been affluent enough to take his children to the country. When she was about fourteen, however, he had a good year and told them they could go. Once the family

The Single Woman

arrived in the country, Antonia found out to her horror that she was to do some menial work in the hotel's kitchen. As a result, she could not really relax to enjoy the vacation. It was a sadistic trick for her father to play, but he was just that kind of man.

Throughout her adolescence, Antonia was severely repressed sexually. Her love life was largely discouraged by her prudish parents. Dates were not much fun, so she kept company mostly with other girls who were in a similar situation. She made a close friend, Trudy, who also became a schoolteacher. Upon graduation, she and Trudy took an apartment together.

Antonia's difficulties dealing with men and sex remained acute. Occasionally she would have a date, but nothing ever led to a durable relationship. She became resigned to the idea that she would never marry. Occasionally she and Trudy would have some sexual contact, though neither one really felt like a lesbian. Antonia, in fact, was more apathetic and asexual than anything else.

Then one day a woman Antonia knew encouraged her to enter the swinging life. By this time she was forty; sexually she was practically a virgin. She began to swing in spite of her strong aversion to men. In the swinging culture that she entered, lesbian love was permitted but not homosexual encounters between men. Antonia began to let herself go sexually, but without much pleasure in what she was doing. In fact, she regarded it as bad and was full of guilt. She found solace in books, especially poetry (her favorite poet was Emily Dickinson).

After a short time, the swinging life became too frightening for Antonia. She would become attached to a man and feel rejected when he left her, although that was inherent in the culture of swinging. She felt herself to be a mere sex object, which led to more hatred of men.

Antonia eventually gave up the swings and returned to a purely bookish life (she was a teacher of English). Her hatred of men remained strong, and she lived out her life as a bitter, disillusioned spinster. The demons of her childhood that led her to feel like a "shitty nitpicker" were too strong.

There is a common myth that somehow the sexual problem has been solved because so much is known about it, because sex clinics are found everywhere, and because sexual freedom and the right to enjoy sexuality are regarded as basic human rights. Yet clinical practice still turns upon one sexual dilemma or another. Not infrequently, as in Antonia's case, women from repressed families hold themselves back so long that when they finally let go and have some sexual experience it leaves them even more lonely than before. Sex without love, like love without sex, is an illusion; the human being needs a resolution involving both.

Olive

A typical example of this problem is Olive, who was brought up very strictly in military surroundings. She was always an obedient girl and obeyed the standard sexual code until she was well into her thirties. She was neither heterosexual nor homosexual, just sexually abstinent, more asexual than anything else. Olive pursued her work as a professor, which excited and pleased her. For quite a while, her main romantic involvement was with a fellow academic. Although she saw him quite frequently, and although he was of about the same age, he never approached her sexually or touched her on any part of her body, or even asked her to dance.

After a brief period in therapy, Olive began to loosen up and have a variety of dates. In some of these, she became involved sexually, but without much feeling for the man and always fearful of the necessarily painful ending. She never married and thus missed out on one of the most vital areas of life.

In her work, Olive was eminently successful; she even wrote several books on special aspects of her subject. However, her success at work did not make up for the absence of love and motherhood. Had she started her liberation earlier, when she was younger and more attractive, she might well have gone further in the struggle for love.

There still seems to be no better resolution of the human problem than a happy marriage and loving family (Fine, 1990b), which I have called the analytic ideal. A start toward this resolution must be made in adolescence. Unfortunately, the crushes of adolescence usually pass quickly rather than move on toward a lifelong relationship.

In many cases, a woman's inability to get married proves to

The Single Woman

be a significant social handicap. Even in this day and age she may be accused of being a prostitute if she goes into a bar. She may receive few invitations from friends because they are afraid that she will make a play for their husbands. Other social handicaps are also common.

Bernice

Bernice was a fiftyish spinster who inspired little enthusiasm in anyone. She gave the impression of being virtually finished with life. Her work, a civil service job, was routine, holding little excitement for her. Her family had died; she had few friends. It was not surprising that she felt perpetually sick and ran from one doctor to another; at least that was better than nothing. She drifted through the rest of her life feeling depressed, sick, unhappy, and bitter.

The Surrogate Mother

Many single women form close friendships with other women and live through them in a sense. Many of these relationships have strong homosexual overtones—as in the case of Antonia. Others are less homosexual; instead, the single woman finds her gratification through identifying her friend with her mother. Essentially, she adopts her friend as a surrogate mother.

Clara

Clara, at about forty, had been an accountant most of her life but could not go far with it. She was unable to become certified or to build a business of her own, so she settled for what she could get, which was routine bookkeeping for a large firm where she felt overwhelmed by a feeling of insignificance.

Clara became friendly with a woman named Charlotte, who was married and had a young daughter. Clara was still dating, and gradually she began confiding details of her private life to Charlotte, turning her into a second mother. Initially, there was no homosexual attraction between them; Charlotte was fairly happily married, and Clara began an affair with a married man who promised to get a divorce and marry her. This promise never materialized, but Clara kept on hoping. Clara's real love, however, was Charlotte, with whom she shared almost every waking moment. She even changed her occupation to one more similar to Charlotte's.

After a while, Charlotte's husband became rather annoyed with his wife for spending so much time on and off the phone with Clara. Quarrels in the marriage began to assume an increasingly ominous character, and Charlotte's husband began to be interested in other women. Analytically speaking, both Charlotte and her husband were having affairs with other women, but Charlotte could not recognize the nature of her attraction to her friend. Besides, Clara was also quite interested in the child. Through her friendship, she had acquired a substitute child she could not have had in any other way.

The friction in Charlotte's marriage grew steadily worse and finally reached a breaking point. Lawyers were brought in, but an amicable resolution could not be found. Charlotte wanted more money than her husband was willing to give her, and the two went to court.

In such trials, as everyone knows, there is a lot of lying and even outright fabrication of evidence. Charlotte wanted to have a strong fight, and Clara declared that she was willing to help her. She claimed that Charlotte's husband had been propositioning her for years and she also said that she once saw him kissing his daughter passionately.

In short, Clara structured her life around a lover, a very close girlfriend, and a child belonging to her friend. She was unfulfilled but not too unhappy. Her work was by no means the most important thing in her life as she had sources of satisfaction in her other activities.

Juliet

A somewhat different scenario appears in the life of Juliet, a forty-year-old dress saleswoman. Juliet had never had much luck with men and had never even come close to marrying or having an affair. Her life centered around her work, which she valued chiefly as a source of money; it gave her no great personal satisfaction.

The Single Woman

Juliet also had a close friend with one child, but in this case the friend, Helen, was a widow. Helen wanted to remarry; a rather weak, passive woman, she was looking for someone to direct her. Her parents were dead, and she did not trust her own judgment, so she turned to Juliet to evaluate the men who approached her. Almost always Juliet found something wrong with them. They were after her friend's money, or they just wanted to have sex, or they were unreliable, and so on. After a while, Helen came to the obvious conclusion that Juliet was trying to keep her for herself and that she was either overtly or unconsciously homosexual. This was reinforced by the frequency with which Juliet would stroke Helen's hair and make comments about its appearance. Suspicious of her friend, Helen broke off the relationship.

Late Marriage

A widespread trend in recent years has been to postpone marriage in order to ensure adequate professional or vocational preparation. According to Blumstein and Schwartz (1983), the average age at marriage in the 1970s for people under forty-five was a full year higher than it had been in the 1950s, and the proportion of women who remained unmarried until they reached the age of twenty to twenty-four had increased by one-third since 1960. The divorce rate had soared, and one out of every three women at least thirty years old was in a marriage that would end in divorce.

Lila is a good example of a case in which delayed marriage worked out very well. At nineteen, Lila was going with a young man who seemed very suitable for her. They loved one another and were happy together except for the fact that he wanted her to get married immediately and have a family. Lila did not want to settle down yet, partly because her mother had married at seventeen and given up a promising career in advertising. Lila's father was a successful publisher, but personally he lacked many desirable qualities. Mostly he liked to sit around, drink, and reminisce about the past. In his firm he was being pushed down, and it was clear that his best years were behind him.

Lila's parents were quite well off, and they assisted her by providing an apartment and the financial wherewithal to go to school. She broke up with her boyfriend, who married someone else shortly thereafter, and pursued her own independent way.

Lila wanted to become a doctor and persisted in her ambition with great determination. Although she had a hard time academically for a while, she eventually made it and set herself up in practice. Once established, she was able to meet a man who was professionally established and concurred in her ambitions. At twenty-eight she married and lived on very happily. The decision to postpone marriage from nineteen to twenty-eight was a wise one.

A problem that many women face is the fear that if they wait until they are fully established in their profession, they will no longer be so attractive to men, and married life will pass them by. This does happen in some cases; in others it does not. Human beings are not made to live alone, and when anyone, man or woman, prolongs the period of isolation too long, the consequences may be serious. Thus, in the popular mind, if a man does not marry before he is forty, he is suspected of being a homosexual, while if a woman is not married by forty, she is suspected of not being marriage material. Like all stereotypes, these may be wrong, but they do exist.

Women who go on to a career, pushing aside opportunities for marriage, may run up against economic problems if they cannot be supported by their families of origin. Hewlett (1986, p. 65) quotes a recent legal decision by a Florida appellate court that denied a forty-eight-year-old housewife's request for continued alimony (she had been divorced for two years) with the statement: "In this era of women's liberation movements and enlightened thinking . . . the woman is as fully equipped as the man to earn a living and provide for her essential needs."

The Wish for Children

To return to the major topic of this chapter, what does the single woman do with herself? I have described a number of reactions: drifting, concentration on work, thinly veiled homosexual attachments to other women, getting to children through girlfriends. The crucial questions are those of marriage and children. Women seem to have less of a capacity for gratification in themselves than men

The Single Woman

do; they need relationships. It is time for a more careful evaluation of our society, in which so many women are denied the natural solution of marriage and motherhood.

The plight of the single woman helps us to focus on one of the really central problems in our culture. There are few cultures where people are as isolated as they are forced to be in ours, and women fare worse in this respect than men. The solution is not to fault men or to argue that women are oppressed (everybody is oppressed in our society) but to create a culture in which women can find normal gratification in a happy sex and love life and still not be forced to busy themselves with routine tasks fit, as Friedan argues, for eight-year-old morons. I have argued this point at greater length in my book *Love and Work: The Value System of Psychoanalysis* (1990b).

By stressing the gratifications of work, many women today, although not wanting to do so, have come to adopt more masculine ideals for themselves. The sex problem can be overcome easily enough by having sex, regardless of the consequences, or by denying its importance. However, women who do that run up against self-recrimination of the most disturbing kind. This is a fact that tends to be denied by the women's liberation movement: the wish to have a child is of so much importance in a woman's life that she cannot wish it away or deny it altogether.

On the other hand, having a child means the assumption of a wholly different way of life, in accordance with what modern psychology teaches. The result is that many women go in for having children and a freer life-style than their mothers had, but with little inner satisfaction. The wish to have a child goes together with the wish to be married, and many women, in order to have children, opt for the solution of a bad or second-rate marriage to having children independently. In Sweden there has been a shift to having the state support women who want to have a child and live alone, but that has not yet taken place in this country. If it did, it would no doubt involve further extensions of social services and social rearrangements.

Other questions are raised by the fact that biological science has managed to keep up with the desire of women to have a baby, even in cases where infertility or age would formerly have made that impossible. Today's methods of enhancing or extending fertility in women (and men) include artificial insemination, in vitro fertilization, use of surrogate mothers, and other techniques. The women of tomorrow will undoubtedly have at least another ten years in which to bear children. The child is a biological event, yet, as Freud once said, "Biology is the land of unlimited possibilities."

Competition with Men

The world of women's work is still too new to permit any definitive conclusions. However, Blumstein and Schwartz (1983), surveying a large number of couples, sum up some of the key difficulties faced by modern couples: partners have to work to make a living, deal with competition, allocate homework, and find time to be together. These challenges turn out to be formidable.

Women who grew up in situations where only the men worked face a special dilemma in adjusting to this new kind of relationship. In a minority of cases, women are not only working but must be earning as much as or even more than their partners. As this trend continues, it will cause more friction with many men because money translates into power, and men are unaccustomed to yielding their power to women. Indeed, men accept a woman's position only so long as it does not challenge their position with other men. Complete liberty for women will be impossible unless men become accustomed to accepting their partner's achievements without feeling threatened. (It should be noted that this competitiveness tends to occur in any couple in which there is at least one male partner. Thus, we find that gay men compete with their partners, while lesbians do not.)

There is a reverse side to this issue that may cause just as great a problem between partners. Men are used to having partners who expect them to be ambitious, and this fits with their own inclinations. The result of this is to make men deeply interested in their work. In the reverse case, however, the man may thwart the woman's desire to have a partner who expects her to be a success at work.

A new question arises: How can a couple create an atmosphere that allows them both to be aggressive in their jobs? If one

The Single Woman

partner does not work, this problem does not arise. However, some couples cannot afford the luxury of one partner remaining at home, and even if they can, the woman may be unhappy in her role as a homemaker or wish to have outside employment. If both partners do work, the couple is faced with the question of who will be the custodian of the relationship.

At the present time, most women are employed, but most of the former wifely roles are still in place. Men are working and living with working women, but they resist changing the rules on which this alliance is based. When we look at housework and find that it is still the woman's job even if she is working full time, we know that men still have not accepted women as true partners. Housework and who does it is a good barometer of how far women have yet to go to achieve full equality with men.

Sylvia Hewlett has written movingly about the plight of the single woman who eventually tries to combine love and a career. Thus, she writes, "Many of us try, feeling as I did in the mid-1950s that in the brave new world, women as well as men should be able to find fulfillment in both love and work. And most of us fail" (p. 137).

That many marriages fail is true enough, and the reasons for this failure have to be sought out. One reason is that the work life as such is seldom as satisfying to the woman as the same life is to the man. A typical example of this is Ingrid (Chapter Four), the nurse who made steady strides in her profession, moving up to supervisory roles and even writing a few textbooks. Nonetheless, happiness remained elusive in her love-starved life.

Profiles of Working Women

Sylvia Hewlett describes the results of a survey she conducted with her own students. In September 1984, she staged a reunion for the women she had taught in the years 1973 to 1981. Those who attended spoke frankly about their lives.

Marion, aged twenty-four, was among the youngest of these women. She held an entry-level position at an investment banking firm, a job she took after completing a master's degree in economics. Marion liked her work and was looking forward to building a career in international finance. She was planning her wedding, and her one great worry was, "Can I make room in this career for children?" Marion did not see herself attempting to have children for at least five years.

By contrast, Laura, who was close to thirty, was beginning to feel pressure to have a child. She was worried, however, that if she took time away from her work to have a child, she would not be able to pick up the reins two or three years later.

Debbie, twenty-five and six months pregnant, an associate editor at a top women's magazine, felt that she had fewer choices than Laura. She and her husband both worked in low-paying fields in New York, and both their incomes were needed to make ends meet. Debbie feared being stuck at home with a small child, and she also worried about losing the equality that she and her husband had built up so carefully in their relationship.

Kathryn, twenty-five and in her second year of law school, described the two most important role models in her life. One was her mother, whom she admired for her ability to do many things well. Kathryn's mother worked before she was married and went to work again after her children were grown. At the same time, Kathryn felt a certain contempt for her mother because she had always sacrificed her work for her family—something Kathryn was determined not to do.

Kathryn's other role model was Laura Siegel, a successful woman lawyer in her late thirties. Yet Kathryn had reservations about Laura's life, too: "'Just fifteen years older than me, she is a high-powered lawyer, a partner in a prestigious firm and well respected by her colleagues. But her personal life is a shambles. She works tremendously long hours and is always traveling. She is divorced, with a twelve-year-old son who recently chose to move from her house to his father's. She clearly has had problems being a parent.'"

During this reunion, Hewlett consistently returned to the question of women's liberation. It did not come up spontaneously—it seemed peripheral to these women's lives—yet she was interested in how it had influenced them. Jackie, aged thirty-three, had been at Barnard when a fairly militant brand of feminism was sweeping the campus. She remembered feeling alienated by the hos-

The Single Woman

tility these feminists expressed toward men and families. She felt that it was time the women's movement stopped focusing on the right not to have children and turned toward helping those women who did want to have children.

An important theme of the evening was the angst associated with being single and childless in your thirties—the condition of a quarter of the women in the room.

Elizabeth, aged thirty-three, was one of the older women at the reunion. She felt that she had a pleasant life, earning a good salary without having to work long hours or commute. Yet she felt her personal life was dying, in part because she lived in the suburbs, where most of the men seemed to be either married or only interested in twenty-year-olds.

Sonia, a contemporary of Elizabeth's, lamented the fact that women her age felt such pressure to have a child before it was too late. Four years earlier, shortly after being married, she had had an abortion, a decision she had come to regret greatly.

Paula, twenty-nine, was an editor in the publications department of a Los Angeles museum. She had taken a cut in salary to move to her present position and was now earning a quarter of what her husband earned. She wondered how she had ended up in such a "traditional" situation, financially speaking, and worried about what might happen if she had a baby. Would she end up in a traditional housewifely role, too?

Clearly, it is no easy task to reconcile a career and family life, and figuring out how to deal with the double burden may be the central problem faced by these women. Hewlett quotes statistics showing that at least half of today's high-achieving women do not find it possible to have children—a much higher figure than for men in comparable jobs.

Thus, the problem looms ever larger: How is a woman to have a family and a career? Many women react with considerable rage toward men, arguing that the burdens of doing both are too much. The mood of anxiety that possesses the young women interviewed by Hewlett is impressive. They feel that they have little time to negotiate the central tasks of their lives, and despite their youth they feel terribly close to failure.

A century ago, Charlotte Gilman wrote, "We have so arranged life that a man may have a house, a family, love, companionship, domesticity and fatherhood, yet remain an active citizen of age and country. We have so arranged life, on the other hand, that a woman must lose; she must either live alone, unloved, unaccompanied, uncared for, homeless, childless, with her work in the world for sole consolation, or give up world service for the joys of love, motherhood and domestic service" (Rossi, 1973). Today's women are struggling to find other options, but the pattern has been set for thousands of years and is not proving easy to break.

10 | The Divorced Woman

Since a happy marriage is the life goal of most women, the divorced woman is triply handicapped—financially, socially, and culturally. Thus, divorce becomes a real tragedy to any woman.

Women could formerly rely on marriage to provide a financially secure way of life. The husband devoted his energies to building his career, the wife to building a home and taking care of the children. Divorce was not frequent, and when it occurred the wife was secure, sure to be protected by the courts. In one famous legal opinion, the judge stated that alimony converts a host of physically and mentally competent young women into an army of alimony drones who neither toil nor spin and become a drain on society and a menace to themselves.

Times have changed drastically. There are no longer many alimony drones. In 1940 there was one divorce for every six marriages, while in 1980 there was one for every two marriages. The prediction now is that two out of every three new marriages will end in divorce (Hewlett, 1986, p. 32).

By the mid-1970s, less than 20 percent of divorces in California involved alimony payments, or in recent language, spousal support payments. The amount of money involved in these payments was quite modest (median award, $200 per month), and one-third of the awards were open-ended, lasting only until death or remarriage. Two-thirds of the awards had a median duration of less than three years. In reality, alimony is no longer much of a deterrent for a dissatisfied husband.

Over the last twenty years, two things have happened to the divorce laws in this country that have undermined the economic position of divorcing women. Most states have enacted some version of no-fault divorce, and most have adopted laws promoting equitable or equal division of property. The main practical effect has been to drastically reduce alimony as a source of long-term income for the divorcing wife.

If the financial status of the woman has been pretty badly shaken, her social and cultural position has never been too good and is still highly inadequate. Women are usually saddled with the care and upbringing of their children, which usually cuts into their love lives drastically. Divorced men find it much easier to remarry than divorced women. According to one study in 1984, the prospects for women finding a second mate deteriorate rapidly, with the odds in favor of men growing from a 25 percent advantage in their twenties to an advantage over thirteen times greater by their sixties. According to census figures, only 18 percent of divorced women eventually remarry.

A woman's fear of divorce can greatly affect the outcome of a marriage. Lucy (Chapter Four), for example, was always talking of breaking up her marriage. Year after year, she would either demand that the house be redecorated or that the couple go to a lawyer and get a divorce. On a number of occasions, Lucy and her husband came within inches of signing the divorce papers. They lived on in this way well into their seventies; he was a meek, submissive man who did whatever she wanted, but she could not make up her mind what she wanted. The fear of becoming a divorced woman played a big role in her constant wavering about the marriage.

When women do divorce, they often turn into bitter man-haters whose psychological problems go much deeper than those of married women. The special problems encountered will be discussed in detail in this chapter; few divorced women escape their impact, though there are always exceptions. Thus, here too social conditions inflict enormous hardships on women.

A case illustrating many of the difficulties of divorce is that of Jill. Jill went through a developmental process that is quite common. The daughter of an unaspiring middle-class family, she discovered after high school that she had no special talents and no

The Divorced Woman

special prospects. So she married, at nineteen, the first man who asked her. It was not a love match, but he seemed a suitable prospect. Two children came of her marriage.

Jill's husband was a steady worker and provided an adequate living for the family. As a person, however, he became less and less interesting. He would sit for hours in front of the television, glued to the latest boxing match or football game. Jill was not interested in these sports, and gradually the marriage began to deteriorate. Jill's husband took little interest in the children, leaving everything in her hands. He did not come alive in social situations; rather, he became increasingly depressed as time went on. Sexually he gradually lost interest in her, not even bothering to take up with other women. He became a little boy again. I have called this reaction regression in the service of the spouse. His mother was still alive, and he longed to be a little boy protected by her motherly embrace. Naturally, in all the battles with his wife, his mother took his side.

Many have called this, quite properly, the "steady Eddie" situation. The husband is a steady sort and makes a comfortable living (though rarely too comfortable because of our economic system). At the same time, he becomes less and less intriguing as a man.

Like many other women in her situation, Jill reacted by finding a lover who was not only quite exciting as a man but also sexually adept. However, he was married. Jill enjoyed the love affair and wanted more of it. She divorced her husband, who was not even too averse to the proceeding, and set herself up in an independent position, ready to welcome the other man. At this point, the lover got cold feet; he wanted only flirtations, not serious commitments like marriage. So Jill was left as a divorced woman, with the task of providing for herself and the two children. She got minimal support from her husband, who just wanted to wash his hands of the whole mess and go back to his mother.

Jill then had to learn to develop herself, which was difficult because she had left high school before graduation and had no special skills to exploit. She took the easiest route, becoming a saleswoman. At one point she discovered that her lover was also seeing several other women, one of whom she knew. So she broke off with her lover and was ready to date other men.

Her parents, who also had to contribute to her support at this point, were very critical of her, condemning her for leaving her husband. They could not understand that there was more to life than the daily grind of shopping and preparing meals; after all, that was how they had managed their lives. Why did she have to be any different?

With her first boyfriend gone, Jill took other lovers and began the sexual experimentation she had avoided in her adolescence for fear of being a "bad girl." None of these lovers lasted; they were all like the first, wanting no permanent attachments. Even therapy did not help; she went to one psychiatrist who often forgot her hours, then blamed her for missing the right times.

The one bright spot in Jill's life was her two children, who were growing up nicely in spite of desertion by their father. After many years of knocking around like this, Jill did contract a second marriage, which, while not ideal, gave her more happiness than the first.

Psychological Defenses

Women often find they have to defend themselves against feeling demeaned by divorce. Their defenses can take many different forms, from psychosis to promiscuity. Perhaps the most common defense—one that feminists tend to ignore—is an exacerbated hatred of men. The case histories that follow will show a range of these responses.

Anger

Kristin, an art teacher, married one of her students after a brief courtship. She was thirty-three and he was thirty-five. Two children were born of the marriage.

Kristin's background was that of the only child of two very regressive parents who married late in life, led a very dry existence, and derived little pleasure from life. She grew up uneventfully, her main problem from adolescence on being her difficulty in having any sexual or love feelings for men. She freely admitted that she had never loved a man but felt no guilt or shame about her difficulties; nor was she aware of her underlying hatred of men.

The Divorced Woman

Kristin's marriage proceeded uneventfully for a time, but eventually Kristin became dissatisfied with her husband. For one thing, he had a problem with premature ejaculation. For another, he came of a very intellectual family whose main preoccupation was incessant bickering about trivialities.

The sexual tensions mounted in Kristin's marriage until the two began to fight. At length Kristin could no longer stand the constant quarreling, which reminded her of her parents' incessant quarreling about inconsequential matters. She and her husband decided to divorce.

At first the divorce negotiations went along peaceably. Then a quarrel erupted about the amount of alimony; he agreed to give her $650 a month; she demanded $750. The $100 difference did not matter very much to either one, but it was the same kind of trivial excuse for contention that each had become accustomed to in their childhood. They went to court to resolve the dilemma.

The couple had a summer house that they had used freely all through the marriage. Kristin's husband started to have affairs and take his girlfriends there. At first Kristin kept to herself, remaining abstinent, which fit in with her sexual anesthesia. Then, gradually, her anger at men began to reassert itself. Kristin knew that her husband was taking women to the summer house, and one night she broke in with a detective and several potential witnesses and found him in flagrante delicto. As a result, the court granted her the $750 alimony she had asked for. However, her husband not only refused to pay the increase but submitted to a jail sentence of six months as punishment.

After the subsequent divorce, both went their separate ways. Kristin lived out her life unable ever to form another relationship with a man; her ex-husband went through a variety of women, marrying several more times. It was a battle between man and woman, carried out in terms of relationships rather than fisticuffs.

Despair

A second common reaction to divorce by women is simply despair. Because so few divorced women are able to remarry, they fall into a state of despair from which it may be difficult to recover.

Harriet, a schizophrenic woman of forty-five (see Chapter Six), was notified of her ex-husband's remarriage on the same day that she received official notice of the divorce. She fell into a psychotic episode, based on the self-disparaging delusion (which came out after much analysis) that she stank so badly that people turned away from her. For example, she thought that when she went into a restaurant, people turned up their noses at her. This was ultimately traced to the fact that when she entered a restaurant she would be quite frightened and would pass gas. People would notice this odor and turn away from her. This made it difficult for her to go into restaurants.

Moving On

The normal reaction to a divorce, as for any separation, is to get over it and move on to new relationships. While rare, sometimes this does happen.

Ramona, at twenty-five, found herself married to a man who was utterly unsuitable for her. He was an accountant who buried himself in his work, neglecting her in the extreme. Her main complaint centered not as much on the sex, which was bad, as on the fact that when he came home from work he would rush into the bedroom, take out a deck of cards, and play solitaire for ten or fifteen minutes. This was Ramona's second marriage, and she suffered acutely because her first husband had done much the same thing.

Ramona's first marriage had resulted in a bitter divorce battle, and she felt bad because the second marriage seemed to be going the same way. She insisted that her husband seek therapy, which he did. In therapy it was discovered that he had had a breakdown when he was in the army and had had psychotherapy recommended to him but would not go. In the face of Ramona's threats to divorce him, he mended his ways and paid more attention to her. This satisfied her for a while, and she stopped complaining about him. It was not, however, a really adequate resolution, and only the course of time could tell how things would work out between them.

A better outcome was seen in the case of Sybil. She was rather promiscuous in her adolescence, with a background of strong sex-

The Divorced Woman

ual attachment to her father and other men in her family. Married at nineteen to an unaspiring clerical worker, she nevertheless decided to make the best of a bad bargain. She was determined to get pregnant, and she even threw a party to announce this fact.

However, the pregnancy never materialized, and eventually Sybil met a new man who was much more outgoing and entertaining than her husband. A love affair started that led to divorce and remarriage. This time, Sybil's sexual life was highly satisfactory, and she was much more gratified in her romantic leanings. The second marriage worked out very well for her; she had two children and returned to the profession she had been in before her first marriage.

In effect, Sybil's second marriage began while she was still married to her first husband. This raises the much-disputed question of the extramarital affair, which has been condemned by moralists, especially religious ones, and promoted by believers in free love, who ignore its ethical and psychological consequences.

Extramarital Sex

The best discussion of adultery and sex in general, after Kinsey, is found in Blumstein and Schwartz's book *American Couples* (1983). Blumstein and Schwartz discuss adultery under the heading of nonmonogamy. They report that a substantial minority of heterosexaul couples (their study includes both heterosexual and homosexual couples) have had sex outside of their primary relationships. They also report that the vast majority of people learn about it sooner or later if their partner has had sex outside of the relationship.

Nonmonogamy conjures up different images for different people. Much depends on the observer's values. For some it may seem a lark: a treat, with little or no bearing on the primary relationship. On the other hand, partners who have experienced what they consider a sexual trespass are often at a loss to know what it means for their relationship.

Couples who have established a nonmonogamous relationship demonstrate that it is possible to create rules that help partners isolate sex with each other from their feelings about each other. This is impossible for traditional couples to imagine, but Blumstein and Schwartz's data show great variation in the sexual rules couples make up for themselves.

A lot of space is devoted to this question because it occupies a lot of space in people's imaginations. Nothing is more hotly and energetically discussed than whether the husband or wife is "cheating" and whether it is right to "cheat" and, if so, under what circumstances.

Interestingly, Blumstein and Schwartz found that wives and husbands are the most deceptive about sex outside their relationship. The interesting point here is that marriage makes couples more deceptive. Couples who marry have traditionally sworn to forsake all others, and it is rare that couples change this agreement, even if they do not always live up to it, and even if open marriage does occur occasionally (but not so frequently as people imagine).

Monogamy remains a strongly held ideal, even when it is not always adhered to. Yet a couple is never completely sure that the relationship will remain monogamous, and constant suspicion that the partner will stray is a feature of most marriages. Although one act of nonmonogamy does not mean that a partner has embarked on a career of infidelity, a woman's nonmonogamy is more likely to be an affair than is a man's. In outside sex, men more often search for variety, while women prefer a special relationship. Couples who lead separate lives have more opportunity to be nonmonogamous, and they are.

Young women today are more liberated about nonmonogamy than women of previous generations. Blumstein and Schwartz cite the example of Sylvia, a twenty-four-year-old student, and her husband Walter, a photographer. Sylvia feels good about not being monogamous: " 'I have a roving eye and sometimes I give in to it. . . . If it's time that doesn't take away from Walter's and my time, I'll let it happen. I consider myself a very sexual person and I need an adventure from time to time. And I think he does, too. But that's all it is—fun and a little bit of an ego thrill.' "

A relationship where one partner loves less than the other makes nonmonogamy more likely. The person who loves less in a relationship has the upper hand because the other person will work harder and suffer more rather than let the relationship break up.

This partner's greater commitment lends power to the person who cares less.

While it is commonly believed that religious people are more conservative about sex, this is only half true. Blumstein and Schwartz found that religious people are as nonmonogamous as anyone else.

Not all nonmonogamy is the same. Some is "cheating," and some occurs in an open relationship. Couples with an understanding about open sex do not always avail themselves of it. Couples with no such understanding are not always safe from it. A successful open relationship has built-in rules, whether or not the couple realizes it. Of all the rules people make in open sexual relationships, the one they emphasize most is keeping sex casual.

Blumstein and Schwartz draw sharp differences between men and women. Women in general are the keepers of fidelity. Sexual compatibility is important to them because they want sex to stay within the relationship, to function as a strong emotional as well as physical bond. Men in general are less confined to the emotional side of sex and are more likely to seek sexual variety. However, men who have female partners become attuned to the female preference for monogamy and do not go outside the relationship as much as they might. Heterosexual men are primarily monogamous. They adjust to the restrictions by designing their sex lives with their partners to accommodate their ideas of sufficient and diverse sex.

Factors Contributing to Divorce

Blumstein and Schwartz identify three primary factors in most divorces: money, sex, and work. They found that all couples who had arguments about money were less likely to be together eighteen months later. They found that the wife's feeling about whether she has the financial resources to leave is strongly related to whether the marriage will survive the early years. "We think that many unhappy wives stay married because they could not maintain a decent standard of living alone" (p. 309).

The way jobs intrude into the relationship is often associated with a couple's breakup. It is primarily the woman's job that is at issue. Blumstein and Schwartz found that when a husband gets upset about his wife's job, the marriage is more likely to fail. The wife's dissatisfaction with her husband's job seems to be critical only among newlyweds. Ambition is relevant, too. The more ambitious partner and the one who gives more time to his or her work is more likely to leave the relationship. New marriages also fail when the husband feels the wife does not do her share of the household tasks.

Dissatisfaction and fighting about sexual difficulties are associated with a breakup. A man's capacity to be tender and expressive is important in keeping the couple together, especially in the early stages of the relationship. Adultery tends to lead to divorce regardless of whether it happens at the beginning of marriage or after many years. Open relationships also tend to break up.

The authors focused their study on young people for the most part, which is probably why they do not consider the problems created by disagreements about children.

It is out of a background of such problems that the divorced woman comes. The irony is that she has to cope with the same problems outside of marriage, this time on her own—money, work, sex. It is no wonder that the divorced woman has a hard time. Some typical reactions have been pointed out above (bitterness against men, despair); others can be mentioned here.

Natalie married right after she graduated from college at twenty-one. Her husband was described as a very dull man, whose favorite amusement was to arrange the pencils in his desk in such a way that they all pointed in the same direction. After about two years, Natalie felt she was totally incompatible with him and got a divorce.

Shortly thereafter, she embarked on a long series of affairs, in the course of which she married several times, each time to an incompatible man whom she divorced shortly after marriage. Her childhood background was one of a distant father, an oversolicitous mother, and a number of men in the family who made sexual advances to her when she was developing into a woman.

Unlike many women in this situation, Natalie had no animosity toward men. After trying out a number of men, she made a happy marriage.

The Divorced Woman

In another case, that of Sarah, the promiscuity had a much less satisfying outcome. Sarah, too, went through a long series of affairs looking for "Mr. Right." Most of these men were either inadequate for her or were casual one-night stands. After many affairs she did remarry, but the second marriage was almost as unhappy at the first and also ended in divorce.

An equally unsatisfactory resolution occurred in the case of Samantha, a forty-year-old schoolteacher. After an early divorce, she experimented sexually with many men; her boast was that she could seduce any man. She was quite promiscuous for a while, sometimes having sex with three or four men in one evening, but then remarried and had a child. Here her real defense came out—she attached herself to the child with such insistence that her new husband felt totally rejected. For example, one evening he invited her to go out for a walk; she said she would speak to him for one hour and then go about her business because her girlfriend was coming over. This marriage also ended in divorce; unfortunately, under her influence the child grew up to hate her father.

Claudia, a forty-year-old woman, was divorced young and also sought compensation in a number of men. She found a bar where men would come to pick up women, and she allowed herself to be picked up often. One night she took a man home, had sex with him, and went to sleep. In the morning he wanted to have sex again, but she was not in the mood. The man was insistent and actually tried to rape her. Claudia managed to call the police, who refused to help, saying, in effect, "You let him in; whatever happens is your responsibility."

At the same time that she was carrying on in this way, Claudia fell in love with a married man. He became the object of her fantasies, but he did not reciprocate her affections. In this unsatisfactory way she went on, on the one hand in love with a married man who did not love her, and on the other picking up men in bars for one-night stands.

Homosexuality

In recent years the problem of homosexuality has come to the fore very strongly. The professional societies of psychiatrists, psychologists, and social workers have all made the mistake of calling homosexuality a "normal deviation." This is in direct contradiction to our clinical experience, as well as to ordinary common sense, and imposes severe hardships on people who are homosexual or are troubled by homosexual leanings.

Sasha was married to a man who administered a large school. The couple had three children. Suddenly Sasha's husband left her—for another man. Naturally a scandal erupted, and he was forced out of his job.

Sasha's reaction to the divorce was twofold. First of all, she began a series of affairs with other men. At the same time she secretly had some homosexual flings. It is plausible that her need to act out some homosexual tendencies was related to the fact that her husband had gone off into a completely homosexual relationship. Sasha also busied herself in her work and in taking care of the children. This went on for a number of years, and she had not as yet remarried or made any more permanent arrangements when last heard from.

To a considerable extent, what happens to the divorced woman depends on the nature of her marriage. If the marriage was on the whole a good one, she can often recover and move on to a new, happier marriage. If the marriage was not a good one, she will continue to suffer unless she becomes aware of her errors and changes accordingly. However, this is very difficult to do.

Roberta came from a small town in Holland. When World War II broke out, she was about seventeen. Since escape was impossible after the Nazis occupied Holland, she stayed on. At first the Nazis treated the Dutch rather well, but as the war worsened, they became increasingly sadistic. Roberta's father was arrested for a civil offense and had to spend some time in jail, which caused the family terrible additional hardship.

When she was nineteen, the Canadians liberated Holland, and Roberta fell in love. She said that before the Canadians came she had never seen a really healthy, robust man. It was no surprise that she married the first young Canadian who approached her. Shortly thereafter, he took her to Canada, where two children were born to the couple.

Soon after the couple settled down, Roberta noticed that her

The Divorced Woman 143

husband often went out at night to unknown places and came home late. Inquiry produced nothing until one day she found a love letter from another man. When she confronted her husband, he admitted that he was homosexual (more correctly, bisexual) and that he had tried psychotherapy several times without success in order to get over it. Still, he did not want to break up the relationship. Roberta pleaded with him to try more therapy and suffered through the marriage.

Even with more therapy, her husband's bisexuality did not change much, and the marriage went on in this way for some twenty years. The longer it lasted, the more resigned Roberta became to her fate in life, at least taking some pleasure in her two children, a boy and a girl.

Finally she could tolerate it no longer and asked for a divorce, which her husband rapidly agreed to. Because he earned very little, there was little child support and no alimony. Anyway, the children were approaching maturity, so the courts would not give her any substantial amount of money.

After the children went away to school, Roberta embarked on an entirely new kind of life, working as a teacher and administrator in one of the local schools. She made new friends, especially women friends, and felt much happier than before. Her wish for a man, however, remained strong.

In order to find men, she answered ads in various lonely hearts columns. As might be expected, she was always very wary, wanting to make sure any man she was interested in had no homosexual tendencies. She dated various men and had a number of brief affairs, but nothing clicked until a gentleman farmer from Iowa turned up. He seemed in every way a personable man, and he claimed to have an adequate income that allowed him not to work much anymore. He introduced her to his sister and other relatives. Everything seemed to be going along smoothly.

Then he proposed to Roberta, saying that because of his business interests they would have to go back to Iowa to live. Nothing suspicious had turned up in the months that they had been going with each other, so, somewhat hesitatingly, she married him. At that, like her first husband, he had a complete change of personality. He began to hit her, and this soon escalated to beatings that hurt her terribly. She spoke to his sister about this, and the sister confirmed that it had happened before with other women. Roberta's husband then began to demand her money because he had very little money of his own. The situation became increasingly unbearable, and Roberta had little alternative but to separate from her husband.

It is true that men often change after marriage; women do, too. How could Roberta have predicted what kind of a man her husband would become? She might have had him investigated, but, although that is heard of occasionally, it goes against the grain for the average woman. Nothing in his premarital behavior suggested that he would turn out this way. Perhaps if she had not had the experience of living with a homosexual man for twenty years, she would have been less desperate about being remarried.

Carroll Baker, a film actress who starred in the fifties, tells a somewhat similar story (Baker, 1983). When she was a young girl, still trying to break into the theater, she met a man who posed as a wealthy hotel owner. He wined and dined her, took her places, and promised to marry her. Then he began to behave in an increasingly suspicious manner. She had about $700 to her name, which he took; then he began temporizing about the marriage. She had to virtually force him to go through with the marriage. Eventually he began to mistreat her more and more, and the marriage had to break up.

Carroll Baker then went on to a Hollywood career. Her second marriage, to Jack Garfein, also went sour, in this case because she did not trust herself to live with him and their two children all the time. Eventually that marriage broke up, too. She says at the end of her book that she has found happiness with a British actor and writer, Donald Burton, but no details are given of the nature of this third marriage.

In sum, the divorced woman, even when she brings about the divorce herself, is often bitterly angry at men, much as the divorced man is often bitterly angry at women. As a rule, this bitterness does not disappear unless the person makes a new relationship that is satisfying.

11 | Recapitulation

I have presented in detail material from the analyses of a large number of different women. Throughout I have taken the position that the goals of psychoanalysis and women's liberation are more or less identical, in spite of the heavy fur flying on both sides.

The analytic ideal, which states that any woman or man attains the greatest degree of happiness if she or he is able to love, has a healthy sex life, has pleasure in general (rather than pain), has feelings yet is guided by reason, is part of a family, is part of a social order, enjoys work, can communicate, has creative outlets, and is free from psychiatric symptomatology, is the core of an analytic sense of normality or happiness. The ideal of women's liberation runs very close to this analytic ideal; it differs from it in practice chiefly in that it places the burden for women's problems squarely on the man, seeing in his persecution the cause of the many troubles that come to plague women.

Furthermore, the elements of this ideal are ones that come naturally to the human being. As anthropologist-psychologist Rohner has shown, they are built into every sensible system that takes charge of human welfare.

We have tried to offer a common-sense classification of women in terms of their functions in society. The basic questions are: What does a woman want, and what are the various hurdles that interfere with getting what she wants? Looked at in this way, the components of the analytic ideal make the most sense.

What is eliminated from this scheme of things? Basically, religion is, with its sour emphasis on the after-life and the fear that

that idea generates. Religion is sharply contradictory to the psychoanalyst's emphasis on pleasure and the things that count toward that goal. Life is for living, and speculation about what comes afterwards does not facilitate living.

Nevertheless, all human societies have had some philosophy or religion that is called upon in times of crisis to overcome the deepest fears to which a human being is subject. These fears are more readily overcome by therapy than by religion. The fear of death is a natural one, but it is not the only one. The unconscious memories of childhood trauma cause more damage to the psyche than death itself.

"Life is for the living" could thus be the motto of all those who profess the psychoanalytic philosophy of living. However, if the course of a life is to run productively, obstacles to its smooth flow must be overcome. Psychoanalysis is in favor of approaches that help the person to prolong life rather than worry about its dissolution, to live in a healthy rather than an unhealthy way. As examples of the range of obstacles a woman must deal with in her life, let us look at three cases in detail: Georgia, Elaine, and Olivia.

At age eighteen, Georgia turned down a marriage offer in order to attend graduate school. As she worked toward her doctorate, she also underwent analysis. After the first few weeks in analysis, she began going five times a week. In her sessions, she spoke freely and always had something to say. At first she concentrated on her family environment; later she switched to more current concerns.

In the early sessions, Georgia described her family circumstances at great length. Her father had been a lawyer, then moved over to a company where he did not play much of a role, just signed papers. Georgia described him as lazy; he would get up late and loll around the house, doing nothing in particular. She did express warmer feelings about her father than about her mother, but they were never truly warm.

Several incidents from her childhood stood out in her mind. One was the whole complex of toilet training, which was complicated by her developing worms when she was about six. She felt terribly embarrassed by this disclosure, taking several sessions to reveal all the pertinent data. Although she did eventually get it out, her embarrassment about the toilet continued for a longer period.

Recapitulation

Georgia's transference never became very intense. She looked upon the analyst as a rather kindly father figure who was there to help her, not get in her way. Disagreements arose continually about the way in which she prepared for her courses. She was always late, and a number of times she was threatened with being dropped from her program. For quite a while the analysis centered on her resentment of her teachers; one in particular was treated with contempt.

The most contentious piece of analysis came after a number of years, when Georgia suddenly would not come to sessions. She would call up and say, "I always come when you want me to come. But actually I want to come when I want to come." This bid for freedom lasted several years. It cost her nothing, since her parents were paying for the analysis. It was really the last gasp of her rebellion against her parents, who otherwise placed no obstacles in her path. In a last gesture of this kind, she handed in a final exam one day late. She then encountered real difficulty with the instructor, who wanted to have her expelled (this was shortly before the end of her doctoral program). However, she managed to avoid being expelled.

In her love life she likewise did not experience any intense transferences. Instead, she was rather cool and indifferent toward men. Sex was easy, and she usually had orgasms, but she did not seem to take to sex very kindly.

The most intense transference in her daily life was to a fellow student named Marjorie. Georgia would call Marjorie up for a date, often on short notice. When Marjorie refused, for one reason or another, she would become highly incensed. "I need you," she would say, demanding that Marjorie recognize her needs.

Another girlfriend, Alexandra, who was in analysis with a different analyst, also received much affection from her. However, when Alexandra's analyst wrote Georgia up in a paper, she became highly incensed at the breach of confidentiality.

After some six years, Georgia finally graduated with a Ph.D. Shortly afterwards, she left analysis. In her case, the transference (feelings toward the analyst) was more negative than positive in the beginning. Georgia was obsessed with the memory of the deworming in her sixth year and covered over this memory by fighting all of her instructors and her analyst. However, she worked out these difficulties and moved on to bigger and better things.

Elaine (Chapter Six) presented an entirely different set of problems. She was twenty-two when she first came to treatment, full of sexual fantasies and with a long series of affairs behind her.

As far back as she could remember, Elaine was extremely sexual. She had vivid memories of an uncle who had flirted with her when she was a little girl, of the men surrounding her father, of the stories her father told, of all the boyfriends she had gone through.

A peculiarity in her early history was her possession of a glass eye. In junior high school she had made up a story about how she had lost one eye when the family moved to Italy during World War II and somehow got caught up in German crossfire. This was, of course, a complete fiction, but she told it to her schoolmates so often that she half-believed it herself. The truth was that she lost her eye in her early school years when a classmate accidentally hit her in the eye with a BB gun. The eye had to be removed, and for years afterwards she went to an ophthalmologist for regular examinations. What she remembered about these visits was that she fainted away every time she saw him.

Actually, Elaine's father was an Italian immigrant who had a dry cleaning store in which the whole family worked assiduously. Her mother was an ordinary housewife who played second fiddle to her father. She did not play much of a role in Elaine's analysis.

Elaine's memories of her childhood were voluminous. As we saw in Chapter Six, she had vivid memories of getting into bed with her parents on Sunday mornings. She also had clear memories of her attachment to her Uncle Mike. When Mike died during her analysis, she was bereft for a while.

Around the age of fourteen or fifteen, Elaine used to walk around the house in her bra and underpants. Her father had a curious reaction to his daughter's growing sexuality: whenever he had to go to the bathroom at night, he would get fully dressed, including putting on his coat and tie. In this period, Elaine's father became an alcoholic. He was unable to work and turned the management of the store over to his wife, who ran it reasonably well. The connection between his alcoholism and her sexual stimulation

Recapitulation 149

of him had never been brought home to her before the current analysis.

As Elaine went through puberty, her sexuality increased. She began to have sex at an early age and continued indiscriminately. After graduation from college, she took a government job and lived in Baltimore for a while. Here she developed the habit of going to burlesque shows. She would notice the girls very carefully, then go home and act out the scenes they had played. This went on for quite a while without being discovered by anyone else.

Elaine was twenty-one and living alone when she began analysis. Her first psychiatrist decimated her morale. His favorite interpretation of her behavior was: "Your head is full of sawdust, isn't it?" She could not understand this interpretation, but let it pass. Then one day he asked her to come on a Sunday. She went and was appalled to find the room full of people; he had asked her to join a group without telling her. Stung by what she perceived as a rejection, she switched to another therapist. For this second therapist her feelings were much warmer, and she stayed with him until she finished her analysis.

Around the time Elaine started with the second therapist, she married a man who was very rejecting of sex, like her father and other lovers. Nevertheless, she stayed with him and even decided to have a child by him. She made a bonfire of her diaphragm, destroying it, but before she became pregnant by her husband she met and fell in love with a man who was more congenial to her. With this boyfriend, whom she later married, her sex life reached the opposite extreme: They would have sex four or five times a day.

Elaine's transference to the second therapist was quite strong. She would talk of how she would like to have sex with him, fantasizing that she was completely nude on the couch. These fantasies, which kept up for quite a while, were handled by simple acquiescence. It soon became clear that she was seducing her father and uncle at the same time. She felt rejected by the analyst but took it in good stride.

In the meantime, her first husband, who actually felt rejected by her, took the initiative and called the analyst for a consultation. This therapy worked out well, in that the man took up with another woman and eventually married her. They had two children and a successful marriage.

Married to her second husband, Elaine proceeded to carry out her wish for children. Two children were born to this marriage, which worked out reasonably well.

Two addenda to this story are relevant. Elaine came to the analyst a few years later to report that she had stolen a bathing suit from a store and been caught. She was now threatened with prosecution. The bathing suit was worth perhaps $25, and she had had about $150 in her purse when she carried it out of the store. Eventually she was let off with a fine.

Several years later she came back again, and it was at this session that she admitted that she had made up the whole story about Italy and the German attack. She also revealed that her first child, a boy, had a sleep problem. He would get into bed with her, and, if his father came along, he would say, "Get out." This sleep problem was handled by behavioral means: The therapist suggested that Elaine put the child's bed next to hers. This device succeeded.

A third case will help to round out this series. Olivia (Chapter Four) was the youngest of four children; the other three were boys. In the course of her analysis it became clear that the whole family was peculiar in one way or another. Her father had been through a period early in her childhood when he walked around on his hands and knees. Her mother had fallen off the porch and been killed, a possible suicide.

At the age of seven, Olivia had fallen down and was thought to have had a brain concussion, although this was never verified. One brother was apparently feeble-minded. He worked for a chess magazine and was killed during an altercation with a fellow worker who was also his lover. Another brother was fixated on gambling. The third brother had become involved in sado-masochistic revenge behavior toward his wife, who was pregnant with another man's baby when he married her. He would say to her, "I married you when you were pregnant by another man; for that reason you have to obey me." This brother had tried to choke his wife a number of times and been pulled off her by his own children.

Olivia first came to therapy when it became obvious that she was not using her potential. When she began therapy, it was clear

Recapitulation

that she was seriously disturbed. She could not begin the sessions, taking ten or fifteen minutes before she could get a word out. She had received therapy before, and some of her resistance could be traced to her previous therapist. He had given up on her, which caused her some disappointment. Although he had trained her to dress properly and groom herself more carefully (she had been sloppy in both departments), he had never really tackled the root causes of her problems.

Olivia revealed a miserable childhood. She had never really had a room of her own, sleeping only in a curtain-enclosed portion of the house. She had been unable to bathe as a little girl because she occupied the room that the bath was ordinarily in. At one point she even revealed that she liked to play with her feces, feeling that they were close to her.

There was a considerable amount of confusion in Olivia's ideation. For example, she would pluck a hair out of her head and suck on it. This was traced back to her sixth year, when she would dunk her hair in a glass of milk and then suck on it. Even though the explanation was clear enough—sucking on her mother's breast—she could not grasp it. Instead, she spoke as if she were three different people—one standing up, one lying down, and one sitting up. Lying down she would always pluck her hair; sitting up never.

Olivia's experience of being raped when she was twenty (see Chapter Four) had many repercussions. At one point she was convinced that one of the analysts in the building was after her. She often had the feeling that when men followed her in the street, what they were thinking of was rape. At another point, she maintained that one of the men in her office was staring at her all the time. When pressed to draw a diagram, however, it became clear that she was the one doing the staring, hoping the man would notice her.

Her transference was difficult to understand and interpret. When she eventually left treatment, she expressed the negative feeling that the analyst really had not responded to her.

For a long time Olivia had no steady boyfriend. After all, she had come to analysis in part because she had worn a slip (instead of a dress) over another slip and was sloppy about her appearance in other ways as well. When she did go out with young men, she would alternate between taking them home and having sex on the spot or saying to them, "What do you think I am? A whore?"

Olivia did not understand many of the simplest analytic expressions. For example, when we worked out that she was not three people, but one, she could not grasp the point to my interpretations since to herself she was obviously three people. A similar problem surfaced when she applied for a job with the city. In the course of applying, she was told by another psychiatrist that she was "schizophrenic," but she made no attempt to understand what was meant by schizophrenia, or what he had in mind, especially since he had asked her almost no questions. At another point, after the wish to be homosexual had been discussed at great length, she reported a dream in which she was kissing the genitals of another woman. When this was pointed out as homosexual, she was flabbergasted.

At times Olivia would insist on infantile behavior. Once she revealed that she would sit in her room and stare out of the windows for hours at anything in sight. She even bought a spy-glass to make clearer what she was seeing.

In one area Olivia was superior—her art work. It was not long after the beginning of analysis that she began to paint and, above all, to sculpt. Her efforts were well-rewarded, and she won a series of prizes in school competitions. Eventually she won a major prize that earned her the envy of all her colleagues.

At the conclusion of her treatment, it was generally held that Olivia was an outgoing, attractive woman in most respects. She eventually married and had two children. In her case, it was a matter of mastering the trauma of infancy, which had been considerable. She had begun analysis indifferent to her appearance, involved with too many men, too fearful of rape. But she persisted, overcoming these problems and others connected with them as well.

12 | The New Woman

What do we want of the new woman? If we run parallel columns on the answers offered by feminists, psychoanalysts, psychologists, and others, the answers would be most enlightening—for all want the same thing. Experts want women to bring up children, to help their men achieve more in life, to realize their creative abilities, to work, to achieve, to lead a rich social life, and more, more, more.

The common-sense reaction to these demands is that women are being asked to do too much. An example is the suggestion made by Suzanne Gordon in her recent book, *Prisoners of Men's Dreams,* that women should set up a National Care Agency, the basis of which should be all the caring professions, at which women are notoriously better than men. Though she admits in earlier chapters that she gets no support from women, who as soon as they become more affluent tend to ignore their less fortunate sisters, nevertheless she pushes her ideas. At one point she says (p. 282), "A National Care agenda would help attract the many millions of men who are now taking care of elderly parents or relatives, or who will be faced with such responsibilities in the future and will need adequate financial and social support. . . . More importantly, if men are not furloughed from the poison of work through shorter hours and extended vacation periods, they will never play a greater role in family life, and women's liberation will remain the stalled revolution about which so many speak with such despair and sorrow."

If the women's movement seems like a stalled revolution, even to its own practitioners, what is the reason, and what is to be done about it? The reason is clear enough: With all the changes brought about by women's liberation, women still feel dissatisfied and frustrated and require a personal hand in helping to overcome these feelings.

In other words, psychoanalysis has set forth its image of what a mature woman should be, but women's liberation has not. The psychoanalytic image is a refinement of the popular wish for liberation and maturity; the women's movement could easily adopt a similar image but does not do so, instead wasting its energy on one utopian scheme or another.

In the age-old battle between the sexes, the women's movement has emphatically denied any hostility on the part of women, though here and there the hostility breaks through. This was the sense of the motion passed at the Seneca Falls convention in 1848—men have everywhere and throughout history ground women down, and this oppression must come to an end.

And what about the children? First of all, studies show that women in the liberation movement on the whole have many fewer children than ordinary women. This is by no means accidental, since these women have renounced family and children in their efforts to gain other ends. Furthermore, feminist theoreticians generally disagree with the psychological measures designed to give children a happy home life, which involves the father as well as the mother.

In the absence of children, or their submergence, the family must necessarily suffer. You cannot have it both ways. If theory underplays the importance of children, the family is weakened or obliterated, since a woman alone cannot handle a family effectively. In the entire range of feminist literature there is virtually no serious discussion of what children can mean to a woman. It is obvious enough that once you begin eliminating part of the family you can end up eliminating the family entirely. Yet how you can have a society without an intact family is a proposition that no woman advocate has ever taken up seriously.

Allied to the problem of children is that of men. What kind of man does the feminist envisage marrying her heroines? These are the men whose interests drive them toward worshipping the woman and being subordinated to her. The battle against male aggression must necessarily take this form; when you do away with male ag-

The New Woman

gression, you do away with a vital part of the male psyche, often reducing the man to a passive, uncommitted being who will do whatever his wife commands. What happens to sexuality in such a family? It is either submerged or absent.

Thus, if the ideals of the women's liberation movement are taken seriously, there is an absence of children, a weakening of the family, and a defect in the man's aggressive impulses. These are obvious effects that every therapist has become familiar with within his or her own practice.

What happens to aggression? It is a special characteristic of women's literature that the problem of women's aggression—toward themselves, toward other women, toward men—is virtually ignored. Yet in a society where premenstrual tension has on occasion been brought in to justify homicide, aggression cannot be far from the surface. If it is argued that aggression is all on the man's side, and that the woman is at worst just defending herself, it quickly becomes apparent that this is little short of a convenient argument to justify women's aggression.

And what about sexuality? Without aggression of some kind, the sex life of a man is seriously blocked. In other words, without some aggression in men, you are apt to have a distorted, truncated view of the sex life.

It comes as no surprise that the women's movement has tended to downplay the natural aggression of man in his sexual behavior, leading to the glorification or idealization of homosexuality, which is now viewed as a natural variation of the sexual appetite (which it most certainly is not). The considerable increase in homosexuality observed on the current scene is to be expected once all the natural outlets for men's aggression are blocked.

That women have historically been the target of men's aggression is beyond dispute; yet that men have been the victims of women's aggression should be equally beyond dispute. The question of which sex is more guilty of aggression is usually considered only from the point of view of the natural differences in strength, but there are other factors involved as well. If a boy is brought up to curb his aggression toward his mother, as most boys still are, it is only natural that he will inhibit his aggression toward his wife or other females. (Incidentally, Freud's observation that men will be able to release their sexuality toward women they see as inferior should be expanded to include the fact that men will release their aggression toward women they see as inferior.)

The liberation movement's cry that women should strive for a reorganization of the social order meets up with a serious objection: How? It is noted that even feminists speak of the woman's revolution as "stalled." It is simply impossible to change one major portion of the social fabric without affecting the entire fabric.

On the other hand, the women's movement has led to an extraordinary extension of interest in the lives of women in other times and other places. We now have far more information on the social, economic, and sexual lives of women in past eras than ever before. All of this, which adds to the sum total of human knowledge, is to the good. To confuse these extensions with desirable social change, however, is altogether incorrect. Some of them may point the way to change, but others may not.

Thus, when the recommendations of the women's movement have been analyzed and the question is put, What is the ideal woman?, the answer is pretty much the same as that provided by general psychology.

REFERENCES

Andelin, H. B. *Fascinating Womanhood.* New York: Bantam, 1980.
Bacall, L. *Lauren Bacall by Myself.* New York: Knopf, 1978.
Baker, C. *Baby Doll: An Autobiography.* New York: Arbor House, 1983.
Bartell, G. D. *Group Sex.* New York: New American Library, 1971.
Blackstone, W. *Commentaries on the Laws of England.* Vol. 1. Dobbs Ferry, N.Y.: Oceana, 1966. (Originally published 1765-1769.)
Blumstein, P., and Schwartz, P. *American Couples.* New York: Morrow, 1983.
Bok, S. *Lying: Moral Choice in Public and Private Life.* New York: Random House, 1979.
Bowlby, J. *Attachment and Loss.* 3 vols. Vol. 1, *Attachment;* Vol. 2, *Separation;* Vol. 3, *Loss.* New York: Basic Books, 1969-1980.
Brody, S. *Patterns of Mothering.* New York: International Universities Press, 1956.
Brody, S., and Axelrad, S. *Mothers, Fathers and Children.* New York: International Universities Press, 1978.
Byron, G. G. *Don Juan, Canto I.* New York: Random House, 1984. (Originally published 1819.)
Canfield, E. K. "Young Women and the Sexual Revolution." In M. Kirkpatrick (ed.), *Women's Sexual Development.* New York: Plenum, 1980.
Chodorow, N. *The Reproduction of Mothering: Psychoanalysis and the Sociology of Gender.* Berkeley, Calif.: University of California Press, 1978.

Chodorow, N. *Feminism and Psychoanalysis.* New Haven, Conn.: Yale University Press, 1989.

Cuber, J., and Harroff, P. *The Significant Americans.* New York: Appleton, 1965.

Darwin, C. *Origin of Species.* New York: Macmillan, 1962. (Originally published 1859.)

Davis, M. D., and Kennedy, E. L. "Oral History and the Study of Sexuality in the Lesbian Community of Buffalo, 1940-1960." In E. Dubois and V. L. Ruiz (eds.), *Unequal Sisters.* New York: Routledge, Chapman & Hall, 1990.

Dawson, B. E. (ed.). *Orificial Surgery: Its Philosophy, Application and Technique.* Newark, N. J.: Physicians Drug News Company, 1912.

Degler, C. *At Odds.* New York: Oxford University Press, 1974.

De Mause, L. *The History of Childhood.* New York: Psychohistory Press, 1974.

Deutsch, H. *The Psychology of Women.* 2 vols. New York: Grune and Stratton, 1946.

Devereux, G. *A Study of Abortion in Primitive Societies.* New York: Julian Press, 1955.

Dubois, E., and Ruiz, V. L. (eds.), *Unequal Sisters.* New York: Routledge, Chapman & Hall, 1990.

Edwards, A. *Shirley Temple.* New York: Berkley Books, 1986.

Ekstein, R. "Daughters and Lovers: Reflections on the Life Cycle of Father-Daughter Relationships." In M. Kirkpatrick (ed.), *Women's Sexual Development.* New York: Plenum, 1980.

El Saadawi, N. *The Hidden Face of Eve: Women in the Arab World.* (S. Hetata, trans.) Boston: Beacon Press, 1982.

Fine, R. *The Forgotten Man.* Cambridge, Mass.: Harvard University Press, 1989.

Fine, R. *The History of Psychoanalysis.* (2nd ed.). New York: Continuum Press, 1990a.

Fine, R. *Love and Work: The Value System of Psychoanalysis.* New York: Continuum Press, 1990b.

Freud, A. *The Writings of Anna Freud.* 8 vols. New York: International Universities Press, 1968.

Freud, S. *The Standard Edition of the Complete Psychological*

References

Works of Sigmund Freud. J. Strachey (ed.), 24 vols. London: Hogarth Press, 1953-1974.

Freud, S. "The Interpretation of Dreams." In J. Strachey (ed.), *The Complete Psychological Works of Sigmund Freud: Standard Edition.* Vols. 4-5. London: Hogarth Press, 1953. (Originally published 1899.)

Freud, S. "Three Essays on the Theory of Sexuality." In J. Strachey (ed.), *The Complete Psychological Works of Sigmund Freud: Standard Edition.* Vol. 7. London: Hogarth Press, 1953. (Originally published 1905.)

Freud, S. "A Case of Successful Treatment by Hypnotism." In J. Strachey (ed.), The Standard Edition of the Complete Psychological Works of Sigmund Freud, Vol. 1. London: Hogarth Press, 1953. (Originally published 1933.)

Freud, S. "The New Introductory Lectures on Psychoanalysis." In J. Strachey (ed.), *The Complete Psychological Works of Sigmund Freud: Standard Edition.* Vol. 22. London: Hogarth Press, 1964. (Originally published 1933.)

Friedan, B. *The Feminine Mystique.* New York: Dell, 1963.

Friedan, B. *The Second Stage.* New York: Simon & Schuster, 1981.

Gallagher, N. B. *My Life with Jacqueline Kennedy.* New York: Paperback Library, 1970.

Gelles, R. J. *The Violent Home.* Newbury Park, Calif.: Sage, 1974.

Gibson, R., and Shaw, S. *Elvis.* New York: McGraw-Hill, 1987.

Goode, W. *The Family* (2nd ed.). Englewood Cliffs, N.J.: Prentice-Hall, 1982.

Gordon, S. *Prisoners of Men's Dreams: Striking Out for a New Feminine Future.* Boston: Little, Brown, 1991.

Greenson, R. R. *Collected Papers on Psychoanalysis.* New York: International Universities Press, 1978.

Greenspan, S. I., and Pollock, G. H. (eds.). *The Course of Life: Psychoanalytic Contributions to Personality Development.* 3 vols. Washington, D.C.: Department of Health and Human Services, 1960.

Hammer, S. *Passionate Attachments.* New York: Rawson Associates, 1982.

Hardy, S. B. *The Woman That Never Evolved.* Cambridge, Mass.: Harvard University Press, 1981.

Harlow, H. *Learning to Love.* New York: James Aronson, 1974.

Hewlett, S. *A Lesser Life: The Myth of Women's Liberation in America.* New York: Morrow, 1986.

Hite, S. *The Hite Report on Male Sexuality.* New York: Knopf, 1981.

Hite, S. *The Hite Report on Female Sexuality.* New York: Knopf, 1983.

Huxley, A. *Brave New World.* New York: HarperCollins, 1979 (originally published 1932).

James, W. *The Principles of Psychology.* New York: Holt, 1980. (Originally published 1902).

Jerrold, W. (ed.). *The Complete Poetical Works of Thomas Hood.* Westport, Conn.: Greenwood Press, 1980. (Originally published 1920.)

Katz, A. "The Paradoxes of Masochism." *Psychoanalytic Psychology,* Spring, 1990, 7(2), pp. 223–241.

Kinsey, A. C., et al. *Sexual Behavior in the Human Female.* Philadelphia: W. B. Saunders, 1953.

Kirkpatrick, M. (ed.). *Women's Sexual Development.* New York: Plenum, 1980.

Lewis, M. "The History of Female Sexuality in the United States." In M. Kirkpatrick (ed.), *Women's Sexual Development.* New York: Plenum, 1980.

Maclaine, S. *Don't Fall Off the Mountain.* New York: Norton, 1970.

Maclaine, S. *Out on a Limb.* New York: Norton, 1983.

Maclaine, S. *Dancing in the Light.* New York: Bantam Books, 1985.

Mahler, M., Pine, F., and Bergman, A. *The Psychological Birth of the Human Infant.* New York: Basic Books, 1975.

Marlow, H. C., and Davis, H. M. *The American Search for Woman.* Santa Barbara, Calif.: Clio Books, 1976.

Masters, W., and Johnson, V. *Human Sexual Response.* Boston: Little, Brown, 1966.

Mercer, R. T., Nichols, E. G., and Doyle, G. C. *Transitions in a Woman's Life.* New York: Springer, 1989.

Morella, J., and Epstein, E. Z. *Forever Lucy: The Life of Lucille Ball.* New York: Berkley Books, 1990.

Narroll, R. *The Moral Order.* Beverly Hills, Calif.: Sage, 1983.

References

Nordhoff, C. *The Communist Societies of the United States.* New York: Schocken Books, 1975.

Parkes, C. M. *Bereavement and Health.* New York: International Universities Press, 1972.

Pleck, E. H. *Domestic Tyranny: The Making of American Social Policy Against Family Violence from Colonial Times to the Present.* New York: Oxford University Press, 1987a.

Pleck, E. H. "Women's History: Gender as a Category of Historical Analysis." In J. Gardner and G. R. Adams (eds.), *Ordinary People and Everyday Life: Perspectives on the New Social History.* Nashville, Tenn.: American Association of State and Local History, 1987b.

Ribble, M. *The Rights of Infants.* New York: Columbia University Press, 1943.

Rohner, R. P. *They Love Me, They Love Me Not: A Worldwide Study of the Effects of Parental Acceptance and Rejection.* New Haven, Conn.: Human Relations Area Files Press, 1975.

Rossi, A. J. *The Feminist Papers.* New York: Bantam Books, 1973.

Schechter, S. *Women and Male Violence.* Boston: South End Press, 1982.

Sinclair, A. *The Emancipation of the American Woman.* New York: Harper Colophon Books, 1966.

Spitz, R. *The First Year of Life:* A Psychoanalytic Study of Normal and Deviant Development of Object Relations. New York: International Universities Press, 1966.

Stevenson, A. *Bitter Fame: The Life of Sylvia Plath.* Boston: Houghton Mifflin, 1989.

Stroube, S., and Stroube, M. S. *Bereavement.* New York: Cambridge University Press, 1987.

Sumner, W. G. *Folkways: A Study of the Sociological Importance of Usages; Manners, Customs, Mores, and Morals.* (A. Lewis and W. Powell, eds.) Salem, N.H.: Ayer, 1979. (Originally published in 1924.)

Weissman, M. M., and Paykel, E. S. *The Depressed Woman.* Chicago: University of Chicago Press, 1974.

Withey, L. *Dearest Friend: The Life of Abigail Adams.* London: Free Press, 1981.

Wollstonecraft, M. *A Vindication of the Rights of Woman.* New York: Norton, 1976. (Originally published 1793.)

Yee, M. S., and Layton, T. N. *In My Father's House.* New York: Berkley Books, 1982.

Zablocki, B. *Alienation and Charisma: A Study of Contemporary American Communes.* New York: Free Press, 1980.

Zolotow, M. *Marilyn Monroe.* New York: Harper & Row, 1990.

PATIENT INDEX

A

Alexandra, 147
Antonia, 118-120, 121

B

Beatrice, 66
Bernice, 121
Bobbie, 67

C

Charlotte, 121-122
Clara, 121-122
Claudia, 141
Cora, 26-27, 29

D

Daisy, 27-29
Debbie, 128
Dorothy, 69

E

Elaine, 74-75, 148-150
Elizabeth, 129
Ellen, 108-109
Eve, 73-74
Evelyn, 103

F

Fanny, 75-76
Felicia, 16
Frieda, 33-35

G

Gloria, 35-36
Grace, 76-78

H

Hannah, 42-43
Harriet, 78-80, 136
Helen, 123
Holly, 83-84

I

Ingrid, 43-44, 127
Irene, 80-81

J

Jackie, 128-129
Jane, 44-45
Jennie, 100-101
Jill, 132-134
Judy, 31-32
Juliet, 122-123

K

Karen, 20, 46-47, 54, 55
Kathryn, 128
Kristin, 134-135

L

Larry, 67
Laura, 128
Lila, 123-124

Linda, 104–105
Lucy, 47–49, 87–89, 132
Lydia, 84–85

M

Mabel, 103
Marilyn, 49–50
Marion, 127–128
Marjorie, 147
Mary, 87
Maud, 68
Melanie, 60
Miriam, 104
Mona, 117–118
Myrna, 54–55

N

Nadia, 118
Nancy, 62
Natalie, 140
Nellie, 101–102
Norma, 50–51

O

Olga, 110
Olive, 120
Olivia, 51–52, 111, 150–152

P

Pamela, 110–111
Pat, 52–53, 65–66, 68, 93–94
Paula, 129
Pearl, 113

R

Rachel, 59
Ramona, 136
Roberta, 142–144
Rosa, 20–21
Ruth, 105–106

S

Sally, 93
Samantha, 141
Sarah, 141
Sasha, 142
Shirley, 59–60
Sonia, 129
Sybil, 136–137
Sylvia, 138

T

Tamara, 61–62
Teresa, 62
Thelma, 102–103
Trudy, 119

U

Uta, 62

W

Wanda, 111–112
Wilma, 62–63

INDEX

A

Acceptance-rejection, in childhood, 25–26
Acton, W., 39
Adam, 86
Adams, A., 5
Adams, J., 5
Africa, women mistreated in, 10
Aggression: and father's absence, 78; and sexuality, 155–156
AIDS, 10, 42
American Psychoanalytic Association, 109
Andelin, H. B., 6
Anger, in divorced women, 134–135
Aristotle, 1
Arnaz, D., 97–98
Attachment, and loss, 99–113
Attention, need for, 90–92
Axelrad, S., 68

B

Bacall, L., 96–97
Baker, C., 91, 144
Ball, L., 97–98
Bartell, G., 49–50
Berryman, J., 107
Blackstone, W., 3
Blumstein, P., 46, 123, 126, 137–140
Bogart, H., 97
Bowlby, J., 18, 100, 110
Brazil, college education for women in, 8
Brody, S., 58, 68
Brown, I. B., 40
Burlingham, D., 71
Burton, D., 144
Byron, G. G., 24

C

California: alimony in, 131; psychologists in, 109
Calvin, J., 41
Childhood: and love, 25–30; and roots of feminism, 19–21
Christianity, and hatred of women, 2, 3
Clitoridectomy, 10, 40
Communitarian groups, love in, 30–33
Competition, and single women, 126–127
Cuber, J., 27

D

Darwin, C., 3–4, 6
Davis, H. M., 2
Davis, M. D., 81–82
de Quincey, T., 108
Death, and loss, 110–111
Degler, C., 41
Desertion, and loss, 100–103
Despair, in divorced women, 135–136
Detroit, domestic violence in, 9

Deutsch, H., 11
Devereux, G., 57
Dickinson, E., 119
DiMaggio, J., 90
Divorced women: anger in, 134–135; aspects of life for, 131–144; despair in, 135–136; and extramarital sex, 137–139; factors contributing to, 139–141; financial hardship for, 131–132; from homosexuals, 141–144; moving on by, 136–137; psychological defenses of, 134–137
Domestic violence, and traditional roles, 8–9
Dougherty, J., 90
Doyle, G. C., 78
Dubois, E., 41
Dunbar, O., 2, 108

E

Education, and marriage, 16
Egypt, clitoridectomy in, 10
Ekstein, R., 70, 71
el Sadal, A., 10
Elaine, 74–75, 148–150
Ellis, H., 41
Engel, 99
English Obstetrical Society, 40
Entertainers: aspects of life for, 86–98; development of, 86–89; maturity of, 92–98; and need for attention, 90–92
Epstein, E. Z., 97–98
Equality, search for, 8–12
Eve (Biblical), 5, 86
Extramarital sex, 137–139

F

Fantasy, and loss, 111–113
Fathers: aspects of separation from, 70–85; childhood relationships with, 25–30; development of relationship with, 70–78; distant, 84–85; in dyadic-phallic phase, 78–80; entertainers for, 86–98; passive, 80–81; untouchable, 81–84. *See also* Men

Fine, R., 7, 17, 70, 116, 117, 120
Fitzgerald, F. S., 108
Florida, alimony in, 124
Freud, A., 63, 71–72, 79
Freud, S., 1, 5, 6–7, 9, 12, 18, 24, 25, 26, 41, 42, 44, 45, 55, 57, 58, 63–65, 71–72, 73, 99, 106, 108, 111, 126, 155–156
Friedan, B., 14, 17, 114, 125

G

Galen, 1
Garfein, J., 144
Gelles, R., 9
Ghana, ambassador to, 92
Gilman, C., 129–130
Goode, W., 30
Gordon, S., 153
Grace, 76–78
Greece, ancient, women inferior in, 1
Greenson, R., 2, 90
Greenspan, S. I., 78
Greer, G., 15
Guyana, communitarian group in, 32

H

Hardy, S. B., 7
Harlow, H., 100
Hate: culture of, 30; and diagnosis, 109–110; toward women, 2, 3
Hawaii, psychologists in, 109
Herzog, J. W., 78
Hewlett, S., 14–16, 58, 114–116, 124, 127–129, 131
Higgins, H., 7
Hildebrand, 2
Hite, S., 21–23
Hitler, A., 26, 109
Homosexuals: and competition, 126; divorce from, 141–144; and untouchability, 81–82
Hood, T., 7–8
Hopi legend, 86
Horney, K., 72–73

Index

Hungary, chess masters in, 11
Hussein, S., 109
Huxley, A., 31

I

India, philosophy from, 95
Innatism, dominance of, 2-6
Intellectual capacities, and traditional roles, 4-5, 11
International Psychoanalytical Association, 109
James, W., 5, 31
Johnson, V., 9-10, 41-42, 73
Johnston, J., 15
Jones, E., 71
Jones, J., 32
Judaism, and menstruation, 9, 68

K

Katz, A., 113
Kennedy, E. L., 81-82
Kinsey, A. C., 10, 41, 46, 137
Kokyangwait, 86
Kris, M., 90

L

Layton, T. N., 32
Legal issues, for married woman, 3
Leonardo da Vinci, 111
Lesbians: and competition, 126; and untouchability, 81-82
Lewis, M., 10, 38-39, 40
Loss: and attachment, 99-113; and bereavement, 99-100; and death, 110-111; and desertion, 100-103; and fantasy, 111-113; fear of, 104-106; reactions to, 103-104; and separation-individuation, 106-110
Love: aspects of, 24-37; background on, 24-25; and childhood, 25-30; contradictory aspects of, 35-37; intentional cultures of, 30-33; as rebellion against family, 33-35; for single women, 116-121; and social controls, 30-33

M

Maclaine, S., 94-96
Maclaine, W., 94
Mahler, M., 100
Malthus, T., 39
Marlow, H. C., 2
Marriage: and education, 16; late, by single women, 123-124; sexual frustration in, 45-47; and women's rights, 3. *See also* Divorced women
Martin, J., 4
Martin, Mrs. J., 4
Masturbation, attitudes toward, 10, 40
Masters, W., 9-10, 41-42, 73
Mather, C., 41
Medical Society of London, 40
Men: attitudes toward women's liberation by, 21-23; competition with, 126-127. *See also* Fathers
Menstruation, myths of, 1, 9, 68
Mercer, R. T., 78
Miller, A., 90, 91
Millett, K., 15
Monroe, M., 90-91
Morella, J., 97-98
Mosher survey, 41
Motherhood: aspects of, 56-69; attack on, 14-17; childhood relationships with, 25-30; and developmentally based conflicts, 63-69; happy and unhappy, 58-63; psychoanalytic view of, 56-58; safeguarding, 17-19; surrogate, and single women, 121-123; wish for, 124-126. *See also* Women

N

National Care Agency, 153
National Wildlife Federation, 92
Nichols, E. G., 78

O

O'Connor, S., 12
Oedipus stage: and fathers, 72, 74,

78, 83; and mothers, 63, 66-67; and neuroses, 26
Ohio, college education for women in, 8
Oneida Community, 32-33
Origen, 2

P

Parents. *See* Fathers; Motherhood
Parkes, C. M., 99
Peck, E., 15
Perutz, K., 15
Physical weakness, and traditional roles, 1, 4
Plath, S., 106-107, 109, 110
Plato, 1
Pleck, E. H., 13
Polgar sisters, 11
Presley, E., 82-83
Prostitution: and traditional roles, 12; and venereal disease, 39-40
Psychoanalysis: and childhood roots of feminism, 19-21; and traditional role, 6-8; and women's liberation, 13-23, 145, 154
Psychology: and defenses, 134-137; and traditional roles, 3, 5, 11

R

Reagan, R., 12
Rebellion, love as, 33-35
Religion, role of, 2, 3, 9, 68, 145-146
Robitscher, J., 109
Roe v. *Wade*, 57
Rohner, R. P., 19, 25-26, 58, 145
Roles, traditional: attack on, 1-12; background on, 1-2; and innatism, 2-6; and psychoanalysis, 6-8; and search for equality, 8-12
Rome, ancient, women inferior in, 1
Rousseau, J.-J., 3
Ruiz, V. L., 41
Ryan, L., 32

S

Schwartz, P., 46, 12, 126, 137-140
Seneca Falls declaration, 12, 154
Separation: from father, 70-85; and loss, 106-110
Sexuality: and adjustment neurosis, 44-45; and aggression, 155-156; aspects of, 38-55; and divorce, 140; and experimentation, 47-53; extramarital, 137-139; frustrated, in marriage, 45-47; history of attitudes toward, 38-42; and older women, 53-55; rejection of, 42-44; and traditional roles, 5-6, 9-10
Siegel, L., 128
Simpson, E., 107
Single women: aspects of life for, 114-130; background on, 114-116; in competition with men, 126-127; late marriage for, 123-124; love and work for, 116-121; surrogate mothers for, 121-123; and wish for children, 124-126; working, profiles of, 127-130
Sotuknang, 86
Spitz, R., 18
Stalin, J., 109
Steinem, G., 17
Stevenson, A., 107
Stone, L., 8
Strasberg, L., 90
Stroube, M. S., 100
Stroube, S., 100
Sumner, W. G., 3
Supreme Court, and abortion, 57
Sweden, single mothers in, 125

T

Temple, S., 92
Tertullian, 2
Thomas, D., 108

U

Unconscious, and reality, 44
United Kingdom: clitoridectomy

Index

in, 40; domestic violence in, 13
United Nations, research for, 18

V

Veblen, W., 39
Vogt, C., 4

W

Wage gap, 114-116
Washington, comparable worth in, 116
Withey, L., 5
Wollstonecraft, M., 12, 13
Women: attack on traditional role of, 1-12; divorced, 131-144; dual nature of, 6; and loss, 99-113; and love, 24-37; new, 153-156; obstacles for, 146-152; older, and sexuality, 53-55; psychoanalytic and women's liberation ideals for, 13-23, 145, 154; recapitulated, 145-152; and sexuality, 38-55; single, 114-130. *See also* Motherhood
Women's liberation: and attack on motherhood, 14-17; background on, 13-14; and childhood roots of feminism, 19-21; men's attitudes toward, 21-23; and psychoanalysis, 13-23, 145, 154; and safeguarding motherhood, 17-19; and search for equality, 8-12
Wordsworth, W., 107
Work: and divorce, 139-140; for single women, 116-121, 127-130

Y

Yee, M. S., 32

Z

Zablocki, B., 30, 31, 32
Zolotow, M., 91